The Rivers and Bayous of Louisiana

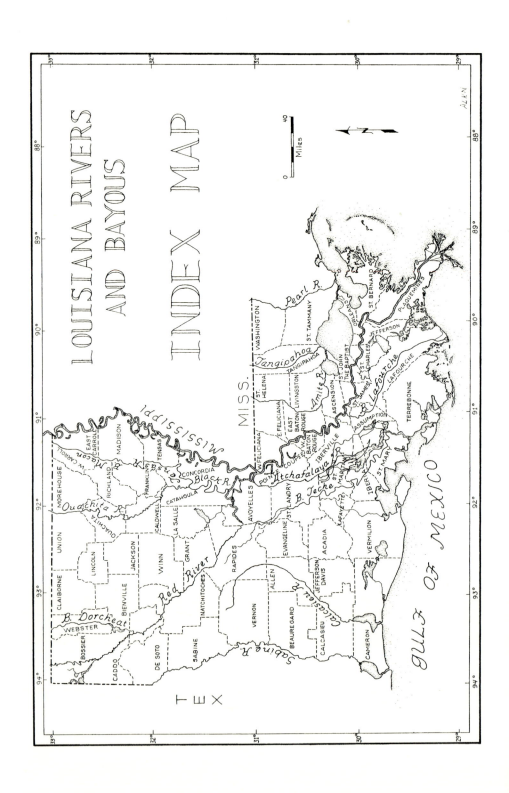

The Rivers and Bayous of Louisiana

Edited by
EDWIN ADAMS DAVIS

A FIREBIRD PRESS BOOK

PELICAN PUBLISHING COMPANY
Gretna 1998

Copyright 1968 by
The Louisiana Education Research Association
Baton Rouge, Louisiana

All rights reserved. No part of this book may be reproduced in any form, by mimeograph or by any other means, without permission from the publisher.

ISBN: 1-56554-437-4

Manufactured in the United States of America

Published by Pelican Publishing Company, Inc.
1000 Burmaster Street, Gretna, Louisiana 70053

Authors

HODDING CARTER
The Amite to the Tangipahoa

ROBERT M. CRISLER
Bayou Teche

SUE LYLES EAKIN
The Atchafalaya

A. OTIS HEBERT, JR.
The Calcasieu

NOLLIE W. HICKMAN
The Tensas–Bayou Macon

MARIETTA M. LEBRETON
Bayou Dorcheat

WALTER M. LOWREY
The Red

SIDNEY J. ROMERO
The Pearl

RALEIGH A. SUAREZ
The Sabine

JOE GRAY TAYLOR
The Upper Mississippi

JOSEPH G. TREGLE, JR.
The Lower Mississippi

PHILIP D. UZEE
Bayou Lafourche

JOHN D. WINTERS
The Ouachita-Black

Editor
EDWIN ADAMS DAVIS

Cartographer
ADA A. K. NEWTON

Foreword

LONG AGO, SOMEONE WROTE that the rivers and bayous were the great architects of Louisiana. Certainly the statement has major elements of truth; for the waterways, which today total almost as many miles as there are miles of highways, have in eons past aided in shaping the face of the Land of Louis, and in historic times have determined many of the patterns of the State's development.

To the Indians these rivers and bayous offered sites for villages and places to fish and were roads of easy travel. To Spanish explorers they were hindrances to movement, hazards to be crossed. To French pioneers they offered locations for settlement and were highways for *coureurs de bois*, trappers, Indian traders, and voyagers of commerce. To the British and Americans they were international boundaries and were barriers to be forded or ferried or bridged in the development of farmland and timberland and other natural resources. Throughout the years, they were determining factors in international diplomacy and played major roles in the rise of economic empires. And all of the men who traveled these streams developed a strong desire to possess and to live upon the lands through which they passed.

Most of the travelers and sojourners who visited and later wrote about Louisiana have praised her waterways and their bordering lands. Alexis de Tocqueville wrote that the lower Mississippi Valley was "the most magnificent dwelling-place prepared by God for man's abode." The Viscount de Chateaubriand wrote ecstatically, in his *Atala*, of the many streams over which nature had thrown "a bridge of flowers." Henry M. Brackenridge described the "coast" (from Pointe Coupee to Bayou Lafourche) as a place where "I could have believed that I was witnessing these paradisiacal scenes of which I have sometimes dreamed." In 1839, Alexander Campbell felt that one Louisiana locale had "an Elysian appearance, and makes one feel as though he were suddenly translated to Arabia Felix, to the environs of Eden, or to some of the spice isles whose Perennial bloom and fragrance form earth's richest types of Paradise that is celestial and eternal." And modern writer H. L. Landers wrote that one stream possessed a "background of mysticism," where "before you is spread the panorama of an immense ribbon, so deep-colored that you gaze upon it in awe-struck wonder."

But some of the waterways, particularly the Mississippi River, have also been bemeaned. One early American settler of the Felicianas, youthful Lieutenant Richard Butler, wrote in the late 1790's that the Mississippi was "the last river God Almighty made, the bottom all quicksand, the water something of the color and thickness of lime and water when mixed for white-washing." A quarter of a century later, British traveler Frances Trollope thus described the mouth of the Mississippi: "I never beheld a scene so utterly desolate. . . . Had Dante seen it, he might have drawn images of another Bolgia from its horrors." British Naval Captain Frederick Marryat called the Father of Waters the "turbulent and blood-stained Mississippi," and "the great common sewer of Western America." And a more recent writer has written of other streams which "tempt" and "haunt" and which cause "a cold fear" to grip the heart.

Here then, along the banks of the rivers and bayous of Louisiana, is found the stuff of which legends and tall tales and dreams and romances are fashioned—and where, also—matter of fact, magnificent history has been and is still being made. Here are the heartlands of Louisiana.

It has been a privilege to have been the editor of the book which presents the dramatic stories of thirteen of Louisiana's major rivers and bayous. The authors have done their work well—the research, the organization, the factual content, the writing of the individual chapters—and the editor has made no attempt to alter their individuality or to standardize their finished products.

Here is historical and descriptive writing at its very best. Here is a book which is a distinct contribution to the historical literature of Louisiana.

The editor is indebted to numerous state and local governmental officials and departments, Chambers of Commerce, and to numerous private citizens for assistance in the publication of this book. Certainly, the collection of an extremely large file of pictures from which the final selection was made would have been impossible without their wholehearted cooperation and assistance; in this regard, special thanks is due Mrs. Edith Atkinson of the State Library. The continuous and active support of Dr. John A. Hunter, President of the Louisiana State University System, is gratefully appreciated. The cooperation of Mr. William J. Dodd, State Superintendent of Public

Education, has been of major importance in the publication of this book. I especially wish to thank the officials and staff members of the State Department of Commerce and Industry, the State Department of Highways, the State Department of Public Works, the Office of the Commissioner of Agriculture, the State Archives and Records Service and its governing Commission, the State Library, the State Tourist Development Commission, the Office of the Secretary of State, the staff of the State Superintendent of Education particularly Mr. Mack Avants, Executive Assistant Superintendent, and Dr. William F. Beyer, Jr., Assistant Superintendent, Curriculum and Instruction, the Office of the Assessor of Catahoula Parish, Mr. E. E. Johnson, Catahoula Parish County Agent, Harrisonburg, Mrs. Henry Jolly of Baton Rouge, the Centenary College Library in Shreveport, and the Louisiana State Wild Life and Fisheries Commission. Appreciation is gratefully acknowledged for the cooperation and assistance of the Louisiana Education Research Association and its membership organizations, particularly Mr. James D. Prescott, Executive Secretary, and the Board of Directors and members of the Louisiana School Boards Association, without whose financial assistance publication of this volume would have been difficult. Also, the assistance of the following Chambers of Commerce is deeply appreciated: New Orleans, Baton Rouge, Monroe, Ruston, Shreveport, Alexandria, Lake Charles, Lafayette, Thibodaux, Houma, Hammond, Covington, Tallulah, Jonesville, Harrisonburg, Winnsboro, Minden, Opelousas, New Iberia, Morgan City, Natchitoches, Bogalusa, and Orange, Texas.

For assistance in the editing process, I am especially indebted to Mrs. Mary McMinn of Charleston, West Virginia, formerly a staff member of the Louisiana State University Press, and to Mrs. Jeanette Hebert, Editor, Bureau of Educational Materials and Research, Louisiana State University. For counsel and wholehearted assistance in all phases of the editing and publication of this book, I am particularly indebted to Mr. A. Otis Hebert, Jr., Director, Louisiana State Archives and Records Service, to Dr. J. Berton Gremillion, Director of the Bureau of Educational Materials and Research at the University, and to Mr. Louis J. Nicolosi, Mr. H. Morris Morgan, and Mr. David E. Watson of the Social Studies Section of the State Department of Education. Appreciation for assistance of a personal nature is due Dr. Martin J. S. Broussard, Dr. R. C. Kemp, Mrs. Mary Claire Davis, and the editor's wife, La Verna Rowe Davis.

Louisiana State University, 1968   EDWIN ADAMS DAVIS

Contents

vii Foreword

Part I: Northeast Louisiana
5   The Upper Mississippi
14 The Tensas–Bayou Macon
21 The Ouachita–Black

Part II: Northwest Louisiana
45 Bayou Dorcheat
52 The Red

Part III: Southwest Louisiana
77 The Sabine
85 The Calcasieu

Part IV: South Louisiana
105 Bayou Teche
113 The Atchafalaya
121 Bayou Lafourche

Part V: Southeast Louisiana
143 The Lower Mississippi
153 The Amite to the Tangipahoa
165 The Pearl

Part VI: Appendix
191 Biography
195 Index

Illustrations

Northeast Louisiana

- 30 The Upper Mississippi
- 31 De Soto Discovering the Mississippi
- 31 Keelboat on the Mississippi
- 32 Flatboat at Bayou Sara
- 32 Interior of Flatboat
- 33 Levee Repair Along the Mississippi
- 34 Laying Concrete Mats, Mississippi River Levee
- 35 The Old River Project
- 36 The Old River Lock
- 37 30-Barge Tow on the Mississippi
- 38 The Tensas
- 38 Headwaters of the Tensas
- 39 Confluence of the Ouachita, Tensas, and Little Rivers
- 40 Convergence of the Ouachita and Boeuf Rivers
- 41 Old Duty Ferry on the Ouachita River

Northwest Louisiana

- 62 Bayou Dorcheat
- 63 Lake Bistineau
- 63 Log Cabin, Old German Colony, Near Minden
- 64 Shreveport
- 65 Shreveport Waterfront, Circa Early 1890's
- 66 Firemen's Parade, Shreveport, Circa 1880's
- 67 Natchitoches, 1864
- 68 The Occupation of Alexandria, 1863
- 69 Logjam on Red River, 1872
- 70 Removal of Logjam on Red River, 1872
- 71 Red River Below Shreveport, 1872
- 72 Red River Commerce
- 73 Red River Above Alexandria

Southwest Louisiana

- 94 Lower Sabine River at Orange, Texas
- 95 Section of Chesapeake Bay Tunnel Under Tow, Lower Sabine River
- 96 Offshore Rig No. 56 Under Tow, Lower Sabine River
- 97 Camping at Sam Houston State Park
- 98 Rice Mill, Lake Charles
- 99 Loading a Barge at Lake Charles
- 100 Tanker on the Calcasieu Ship Channel
- 101 Tour of the Lake Charles Port

South Louisiana

- 129 Oil Barge on Lower Bayou Teche
- 130 "The Shadows," New Iberia
- 131 Blessing of the Shrimp Fleet, Morgan City
- 132 Trappers, Lower Atchafalaya
- 133 The Trapper, Coastal Marshes Along the Lower Atchafalaya
- 134 Oil Rig, Bayou Lafourche
- 135 Icing a Trawler, Lower Bayou Lafourche
- 136 Bayou Lafourche at Golden Meadow
- 137 Old-time Oyster Bar, Bayou Lafourche
- 138 Oyster Shells, Lower Bayou Lafourche
- 139 Commercial Fishing Trap, Lower Bayou Lafourche
- 140 "Rienzi," Near Thibodaux

Southeast Louisiana

- 172 Baton Rouge, Early 1860's
- 172 New Orleans Levee, Early 1870's
- 173 New Orleans, 1862
- 174 New Orleans Wharves, 1890's
- 175 Loading Cotton at New Orleans
- 176 The Port of New Orleans
- 177 Greater New Orleans Bridge
- 178 Vieux Carre, New Orleans
- 179 Sulphur Plant on the Lower Mississippi
- 180 Estuaries of the Mississippi
- 181 Southwest Pass, Mouth of the Mississippi
- 182 "Mud Lump," Mouth of the Mississippi
- 183 Meandering Lower Amite River
- 184 Amite River Diversion Channel
- 185 Amite River Near French Settlement
- 186 The Tangipahoa River
- 186 The Lower Pearl River
- 187 Paper Mill, Bogalusa

Maps

Frontispiece Index Map

Facing page
- 8 Upper Mississippi
- 16 The Tensas
- 24 Ouachita and Black
- 49 Bayou Dorcheat
- 59 The Red River
- 80 The Sabine
- 88 The Calcasieu
- 108 Bayou Teche
- 116 The Atchafalaya
- 124 Bayou Lafourche
- 149 Lower Mississippi
- 158 Amite and Tangipahoa
- 169 Pearl River

The Rivers and Bayous of Louisiana

Part I | *Northeast Louisiana*

The Upper Mississippi

By Joe Gray Taylor

THE MISSISSIPPI RIVER leaves Arkansas behind just south of the thirty-third degree of north latitude and, for about 175 miles (much more by the meandering path of the channel), flows between the State of Mississippi to the east and Louisiana to the west. Coming in from the northwest, the Red River joins the Mississippi almost exactly opposite the boundary between Wilkinson County, Mississippi, and West Feliciana Parish, Louisiana, on the east bank. As it moves down to its meeting with the Red, the Father of Waters passes Lake Providence, Tallulah, St. Joseph, Vidalia, and the Cocodrie Swamp on the Louisiana side, historic Vicksburg and Natchez on the Mississippi side. After absorbing Red River, the Mississippi flows southeastward, passing Morganza, New Roads, and St. Francisville, some fifty more air-line miles to Baton Rouge, the capital of Louisiana and the head of ocean navigation.

A glance at the map shows that this mighty stream has been a restless one. The beautiful lakes on the west, Lake Providence, Lake Bruin, Lake St. John, Lake Concordia, Old River, and False River are all former beds of the Mississippi, left behind when the channel shifted. Even in the last century, the river has changed its course often enough to make it difficult, sometimes, to say exactly where the boundary between Louisiana and the State of Mississippi is to be found. Between St. Joseph and Tallulah is Davis Island, now on the west side and almost completely surrounded by Louisiana soil. But before the Civil War it lay on the east side, and was the site of a great plantation owned by Joseph Davis, brother of Jefferson Davis. Davis Island is still a part of Mississippi, as is another tract of land just north of Vidalia. The town of Waterproof, in Tensas Parish, has been moved four times in its history to prevent its being devoured by the restless river. As of today, the Mississippi has not escaped the levees that restrain it for almost a third of a century, but when its waters lap near the top of the levees, Louisianians living on the low alluvial lands to the west are rightfully fearful.

In Louisiana very few Indians lived along the Mississippi north of Baton Rouge before the white man came. A few Tunicas, under various names, probably less than five hundred of them, dwelt in the northeastern corner of the state, and scattered parties of Natchez, who had a sizable village on the east bank where the city of Natchez now stands, pushed into the great forests to the west.

In the year 1542, Hernando de Soto and his followers were the first white men to gaze upon the Mississippi River. We do not know exactly where these Spanish explorers crossed, but it was probably from Mississippi into Louisiana as the maps are now drawn. De Soto died to the west, and the survivors of his company built boats, made their way downriver to the Gulf of Mexico, and finally came to the Spanish settlements in Mexico.

Forty years later, René Robert Cavelier, the Sieur de la Salle, led a party of French and Indians down the Mississippi to its mouth. We know that they visited the Tensas, Natchez, and other Indians on their way downstream. La Salle opened up a route followed by French traders, especially Henri de Tonti, and these voyageurs seem to have been very familiar with the Mississippi by the time the Louisiana colony was established on the Gulf Coast in 1699. By that time, also, it was quite probable that traders from South Carolina had visited the river north of Baton Rouge.

As the French consolidated their position in the lower Mississippi Valley, settlements were established at Natchez, Lake Providence, Baton Rouge, and Pointe Coupee, but these settlements remained small through the eighteenth century. When Spain took possession of Louisiana after the French and Indian War, more settlers arrived, encouraged by liberal grants of land along the Mississippi. One of these grants was to Joseph Vidal, and the name he gave to his settlement, Concordia, became the name of the parish, and the parish seat, Vidalia, took its name from Vidal. Baton Rouge and Natchez became British after this war, so the Mississippi was the boundary between two great empires.

When the thirteen British colonies won their independence, Spain, which had fought against the English, regained possession of West Florida, including Baton Rouge and Natchez, but the new United States claimed Natchez and eventually made good its claim. During the last years of the eighteenth century, the waters of the Mississippi bore a new kind of traffic, rafts and flatboats which were little more than rafts, carrying fierce-looking American frontiersmen from the lands along the Ohio and Cumberland rivers. The Louisianians called them all "Kaintucks" and had as little to do with them as possible.

With the Louisiana Purchase of 1803, the west bank of the upper

Mississippi became American, although Spain retained West Florida, administered from Baton Rouge, on the east bank. But many Americans had settled in West Florida, and in 1810 they carried out an almost bloodless revolution. From that time on, except for the years of the Civil War, the Mississippi flowed through United States territory from its source to its mouth.

With every passing year, the Mississippi bore more American traffic. When the rafts and flatboats from upriver reached New Orleans, the owners sold their goods, then sold the timber from which their craft were built, and made their way back north on foot or on horseback. The return trip was a perilous one because murderous outlaws haunted the river and preyed upon travelers. Among these cutthroats were the Harpe brothers, "Judge" Samuel Mason, and the infamous John A. Murrell. Indeed, it was not until the 1830's that a reasonable degree of law and order was achieved along the Mississippi north of Baton Rouge.

Some traders from upriver began to avoid the land journey home by floating down to New Orleans in clumsy keelboats. The voyage down, with the current, was not so difficult, but returning upstream was a laborious process. Sometimes the crew propelled the boat by "poling," walking from one end of the deck to the other pushing on poles thrust into the bottom; but where it was necessary to fight the current, they might have to go ashore, tie a line to a tree upstream, and pull the boat forward, repeating this process again and again.

In 1812, people living along the river heard a new sound, the huffing and puffing of a steam engine. The *New Orleans,* built in Pittsburgh, was making its way downstream to the city for which it was named. Unfortunately, this first Mississippi River steamboat had engines too weak to push it against the current, so the rest of its days were spent on the lower river. But in 1816 the *Enterprise* went down and then fought its way back up. The *New Orleans* and the *Enterprise* were simply keelboats equipped with a steam engine, but in just a few years the true riverboat, a high-pressure steam engine mounted on a hull of such shallow draft that it could "steam across a heavy dew," made its appearance. The rapid transportation provided by the steamboat contributed much to the prosperity of the villages and plantations of Louisiana.

Natchez had become a thriving village by the time of the American Revolution, and the coming of extensive cotton cultivation, made possible by the invention of the cotton gin, brought expanded prosperity. Cotton farming spread rapidly into the Felicianas. In the meantime, Etienne de Boré had learned how to make sugar from Louisiana cane, and the cultivation of this crop expanded around Baton Rouge and on north on the west bank to Red River. It quickly became apparent that the plantation, worked by slave labor, provided the most efficient unit for cultivating sugar and cotton.

Settlement of the lands on the west bank of the Mississippi above Red River proceeded until the 1830's; but, during the boom years of Andrew Jackson's presidency, high prices for cotton and increasing land values persuaded many venturesome souls to open plantations on the Louisiana side of the river. These lands, when cleared, were immensely productive of cotton and corn. The depression which began in 1837 slowed, but did not halt, settlement; and, by the late 1840's, practically all the well-drained lands from the Arkansas border to Cocodrie Swamp were taken up with flourishing cotton plantations. South of Red River, the sugar plantations in Pointe Coupee and West Baton Rouge parishes continued to prosper, and in the Felicianas cotton, interspersed with sugarcane, was the chief crop.

The fortunate men who owned and operated these plantations enjoyed, with their families, a way of life which was not to last long. Most of them lived on their own lands, though there were some who resided in Natchez, Vicksburg, or New Orleans and left the direction of their plantations to an overseer. Few great mansions were built; the country was too new for ostentatious display, but the planters did have, in the main, commodious and comfortable homes. In the Felicianas, where settlements were older, there were some true mansions. The planter families were renowned for their wealth, their political influence, and their hospitality.

Most Louisiana plantations along the Mississippi north of Baton Rouge had fewer than 50 Negro slaves, but scores had more than 100, and a few had almost 200. Among these slaves were blacksmiths, carpenters, coopers, house servants, and field hands. Often the house servants were almost members of the planter's family, and the skilled workers had positions of importance and trust on the plantation. But the vast majority of the Negroes were field hands, whose task was to plow, plant, hoe, and harvest the bountiful crops of sugar and cotton. As slaves they had little to gain by hard work, so strict supervision and, sometimes, severe treatment were necessary to keep them at their tasks. This was the harsh side of slavery, which caused many Louisianians to believe privately what the northern abolitionists said publicly, that slavery was a great evil.

When the Civil War came, the sugar plantations in Pointe Coupee and West Baton Rouge parishes were hardly fifty years old, and the cotton plantations along the Mississippi north of Red River had, most of them, been forest thirty years before. The Civil War was to bring an abrupt end to a way of life; the land and the people would remain, but the relationship would be very different when the fighting had ended.

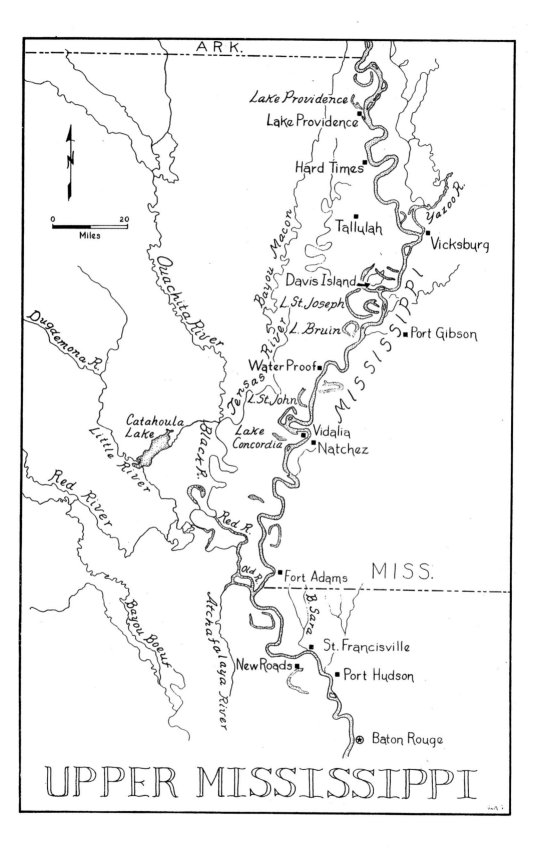

The Mississippi was crucial to both sides in this war. The North captured Memphis and New Orleans early in the struggle. For all practical purposes, the Confederacy by 1863 was left in possession only of a section of the river between Vicksburg and Port Hudson. If the northern armies could gain control of this portion of the river, the South would be cut in two, and supplies from western Louisiana and Texas could not reach the Confederate armies in the East. Therefore, the capture of Vicksburg and Port Hudson became the great objective of the Union forces in the West; the retention of these two posts was the object of their Confederate opponents.

Seldom have more determined adversaries faced one another. General Ulysses S. Grant, the Union commander, tried to advance overland to Vicksburg from Memphis, but this proved impossible. The river provided an admirable supply line, but Vicksburg, on a high bluff overlooking a great bend in the Mississippi, proved impregnable to attack from the river. Therefore, Grant moved his army downriver and encamped on the Louisiana side opposite and above Vicksburg. He tried to dig a canal across the base of the great bend before Vicksburg, hoping that the channel of the river might follow the canal. But this task was not completed before high waters put an end to the work. In another attempt to get around the guns of Vicksburg, Grant tried to turn the Mississippi into Lake Providence and thus open a route into the Red River. This scheme also proved impractical. He made another effort to move troops to the rear of the city by way of Yazoo Pass during the high-water stage of the river, but was again unsuccessful.

By the spring of 1863, Grant had to find some way to attack Vicksburg or retreat all the way north to Memphis. When the roads were passable, he marched his troops down the west bank of the river to Hard Times, Louisiana, and the Union Navy ran gunboats and transports past the Vicksburg batteries. Grant then crossed the Mississippi, captured Port Gibson, and marched on Jackson. Once Jackson was in his hands, he turned back west against Vicksburg. Siege lines were drawn about the city; and finally, on July 4, 1863, the Confederate defenders surrendered.

In the meantime General Nathaniel P. Banks, whose headquarters were in New Orleans, had moved against Port Hudson. Here also there was heavy fighting. The Confederate garrison gave a good account of itself, but, as at Vicksburg, the superior numbers and equipment of the northern forces gradually decided the issue. The defenders of Port Hudson might possibly have held out longer, but when news arrived of the fall of Vicksburg, resistance became useless. Surrender terms were agreed upon, and the last Confederate position on the Mississippi passed into Union hands. With the fall of these two forts, the Confederacy was mortally wounded; the end could be delayed, but it could not be avoided.

The people along the river saw these events from different points of view. To the planters and their families, the expectation of victory gave way to fear, and fear in time gave way to despair. Some remained on their lands; others fled westward, many all the way to Texas, taking their slaves with them. The Negroes took a very different view of the invading forces. Few instances can be found of their harming, or even being discourteous to, their masters, but when the Federal armies came near, vast numbers of them ran away. Some, after sampling life about an army camp, returned home, but others did not. Thousands of the younger Negro men enlisted in the Union army, and they rendered a good account of themselves at the siege of Port Hudson.

When the war ended, the destruction to be seen on every side along the Mississippi from Vicksburg to Baton Rouge was probably as extensive as was to be found anywhere in the South. Most of the plantation houses had been burned, and those that remained had been stripped of their furnishings. The planters had invested most of their wealth in slaves, and this investment was lost forever. The land remained, but the tools, the livestock, and the labor had disappeared during the war. For most of the planters, life had to begin again under new and unfamiliar conditions. Some were not equal to the struggle, and many plantations changed hands. Not a few of them were bought up by Northerners who had liked what they saw in the South during the war.

For the white Louisianians who lived along the Mississippi above Baton Rouge, the ten years that followed the Civil War were, in some respects, harder to bear than the years of destruction. Under the Reconstruction Acts passed by Congress in 1867, a state government made up largely of Negroes and Northerners who had moved south—carpetbaggers—was elected. Under this Republican regime, taxes were much higher than before the war, and planters who had barely managed to avoid bankruptcy found this added burden hard to bear. The Reconstruction years were especially galling to whites in the parishes along the upper Mississippi, because in this region of great plantations, Negroes made up a vast majority of the population.

One serious problem was solved during these years. Many people were puzzled when slavery ended as to just how labor for the plantations was to be secured. The solution to this problem was found in sharecropping, a system under which the planters provided land, tools, and livestock, and the Negro (or the poorer white man) provided his labor. When the harvest was in, the earnings from the sharecropper's acres were divided equally between cropper and landlord. This was far from a perfect system, but it is hard to see what else could have worked. Without it, the rich lands along the Mississippi from Lake Providence to Baton Rouge might well have reverted to wilderness. Political Reconstruction finally ended in

1876 with the election of a Democratic state government, but the sharecrop system survived well into the twentieth century.

The years following the Civil War were the time of glory for the steamboat on the Mississippi River. Some of these craft were veritable floating palaces, bearing such famous names as the *Natchez,* the *Grand Republic,* the *Eclipse,* and the *Robert E. Lee.* Accidents were not infrequent as boilers burst on the high-pressure steam engines or the hazards of the river tore holes in the fragile hulls, but danger only added spice to river travel. The steamboat era came to an end because the railroads along the shore could deliver goods and passengers to their destination so much more rapidly. It should be pointed, out, however, that although the railroads put an end to the romantic river steamers, they did not by any means put an end to river traffic. Today the prosaic tug, with its tow of barges, moves more tonnage up and down the Mississippi in a year than the steamboats, at the height of their glory, could have moved in several years. But the showboat, the gilded saloon, the river gambler, and the excited passengers waiting at the dock are gone forever.

The last years of the nineteenth century and the first third of the twentieth were not easy years for the people along the upper Mississippi. Most times were bad times, and good times were never very good. Some planters grew wealthy, but just as many faced bankruptcy. The vast majority avoided these extremes, but they often felt that they were running as hard as they could to stay in the same place. The sharecropper had some good years, but more often he began the year in debt and ended it deeper in debt. The people in the towns, dependent upon the plantations for their prosperity, were just as buoyed up by a rise in the price of cotton or sugar, and just as cast down by a fall, as the planter or sharecropper.

The greatest blow to the economy of the region came with the great depression of 1929, but this catastrophe also brought the beginning of many changes for the better. Limited acreage for cotton and sugar under the Federal farm programs ended the usefulness of many sharecroppers. At the same time, the beginnings of mechanization were destroying the very foundations of the system. And government payments to landowners and better prices for sugar and cotton were providing capital with which more machines could be purchased. During World War II a migration of people to the cities of the North and South was a further incentive. As a result, the growing of cotton and sugar along the Mississippi today is a highly efficient mechanized operation. Tractors do the work once done by mules, and complicated but effective machines plant, cultivate, and harvest the crops. Chemicals destroy insect pests, control grass, and provide effective fertilizers. One man, with these machines and chemicals, now can do the work once done by several families of sharecroppers. The provision of these implements, and their servicing, adds to the prosperity of the people of the towns.

Perhaps more important, cotton and sugar are no longer the sole source of wealth along the banks of the Mississippi. Many acres once devoted to row crops are now profitably used for cattle grazing, and the cattle are far superior to those of a few decades ago. Industry is beginning to make its appearance in the larger cities of the region north of Baton Rouge. Oil wells are found here and there, especially in Concordia Parish. Finally, the recreational resources of this area have been discovered and are used more and more. Hunting is excellent, and the lakes of East Carroll, Tensas, Madison, Concordia, and Pointe Coupee parishes provide fishing equal to any in the world.

The Mississippi still rolls on. It has less freedom now, as levees rise to protect the lowlands, and as the structures of the United States Army Corps of Engineers restrict its custom of changing course at the slightest whim. The traveler sees the Mississippi now only when he crosses a bridge at Vicksburg, Natchez, or Baton Rouge, or when he makes a special effort. But it is still there, the most majestic stream on the continent, subject of legend and song, flowing out of the past and into the future.

The Tensas–Bayou Macon

By NOLLIE W. HICKMAN

THE TENSAS BASIN is a flat alluvial plain formed over a period of countless ages by the mighty Mississippi River. With its northern boundary in Arkansas, the basin extends south and southwestward to the Black and Ouachita rivers, and westward from the Mississippi to the highlands on the west bank of Bayou Macon. In its long journey to the Gulf of Mexico, the Father of Waters deposited fertile soil, built up natural levees, and dug many channels as it sought new paths to the sea; oxbow-shaped lakes and bayous in the basin were once the main stream of the Mississippi.

The land lying between Bayou Macon and the Mississippi, lower than the natural levees of the two streams, formed a depression that was inundated in periods of flood. During the disastrous flood of 1927, the basin was from four feet to twelve feet underwater, and one could travel by boat from Vicksburg west to Monroe, a distance of eighty miles.

The depression was drained by two main streams, the Tensas River and Bayou Macon. The Tensas originated in Lake Providence, an oxbow lake, and flowed southward, joining the Ouachita and Little rivers to form the Black River. In the course of its 315-mile journey the Tensas is joined by a number of bayous, the most important being Bayou Macon.

After traveling from Jefferson County, Arkansas, for 250 miles, Bayou Macon joins the Tensas 42 miles before the latter reaches the Black River. Together the two streams and their tributaries drain 3,000 square miles, 95 percent of which lies in the Tensas Basin. In their upper reaches, both Bayou Macon and the Tensas are narrow and shallow. But both streams become deeper and broader after being joined by their tributaries. Though varying with the seasons, the channel of the Tensas near its mouth has a width of from 100 feet to 200 feet and a depth ranging from 2 feet to 6 feet. Heights of the riverbanks are from 40 feet to 60 feet.

The twisting, meandering streams pass through some of the most fertile soils and what was once one of the finest hardwood forests in America. On the natural levees built up by constant overflows once grew cottonwood, sycamore, black willow, hackberry, honey locust, and a variety of oaks. So close to the water grew the trees that their overhanging branches and bent trunks were formidable obstacles to navigation. Farther back behind the natural levees in the low, wet lands were cypress brakes, tupelo, gum, swamp red maple, two species of ash, water oak, and other valuable trees. Almost all of the basin was covered by a vast sea of dense, impenetrable bamboo-type cane overshadowed by towering gums, mighty oaks, and picturesque cypresses. Faced by the green, uncompromising wall, early settlers avoided the dense forests and low, wet lands.

In the virgin forests were deer, bears, panthers, wolves, beavers, otters, and other animals. Bayous and rivers teemed with fish. Both the forests and streams made important contributions to the economy, as they still do today.

To write the story of an American river is to tell the saga of the growth of a region. It was by means of streams that explorers and traders pushed inland into America. Rivers formed the principal highway of trade and communication. The natural pulse moving the pioneer forward was the rhythm of flowing water. Although small compared to other American streams, the Tensas and Bayou Macon were avenues of opportunity and beckoning roads to adventurers.

When white men first appeared on the edge of the basin, except for a small branch of the Natchez tribe, the Tensas, no Indians permanently occupied the region. At an earlier period Indian mounds were built in various locations throughout the basin. Perhaps the periodic floods and the unhealthy lowlands made permanent occupancy impossible. Except for hunting parties, the wildernesses along the rivers were undisturbed until white men came.

The first white men to see the Tensas River were Hernando de Soto and his followers when they passed the mouth of the stream en route to the Mississippi. After De Soto's brief glimpse, 140 years elapsed before other white men intruded. Areas drained by Bayou Macon and the Tensas remained largely unknown and unexplored until well into the eighteenth century. Except for a few Indian clearings, nothing disturbed the silence of a primeval wilderness.

The French, during their occupation of Louisiana, made no permanent settlements on Bayou Macon or on the Tensas. Hunters and trappers pursued the beaver, bear, and deer, but left no lasting imprint. Successors of the French, the Spanish, were also slow to develop their vast possessions. Not until the close of the eighteenth century were steps taken by the Spanish to encourage settlement. Numerous land grants were made in Concordia Parish and along the banks and at the mouth of the Tensas River. Unsuccessfully, the Spanish tried to build a wall against aggressive American migration.

During the last years of Spanish occupation, settlers in small numbers crossed the Mississippi and built homes in the basin. This influx was due in part to the invention of the cotton gin. Immediately following acquisition of Louisiana by the United States, the tide of immigration increased, but was not to assume important proportions until after 1830. Among the families who came before 1830 were the Osborns, Gilberts, Wards, Watsons, and many others. At Swampers, a village on the Tensas, the Webb Parker and Ennos Laborde families settled in 1802 and 1803.

Farming was not always the principal occupation of the early settlers, many of whom depended mainly on hunting and fishing. The few acres they farmed were enclosed by hewn palings to protect their crops from roving livestock. Except for a few plantations carved out of the wilderness by slave labor, a twenty-acre field was unusual in the first phase of basin settlement.

When John James Audubon came down the Mississippi River in 1821, the naturalist observed squatters settling on the west bank of the river. His conception of the squatter was different from the prevailing views of his time regarding this class of people. The squatters, according to Audubon, had learned of the fertile soil, abundance of game, and the ready market for goods at the mouth of the river. Of even greater weight was the opportunity to settle on fertile land for a number of years without purchase, tax, or rent.

Soon after the arrival of the squatter family, a small patch of land was cleared and a crude cabin erected. Bells were attached to the cattle and they were turned loose in the woods. Looms were mounted, and spinning wheels soon furnished yarn to provide apparel suitable for the climate.

Before the coming of frost in November, the unacclimated family was attacked by fever. But the sickly season soon passed, and with a diet of bear meat and venison the family regained its physical strength. During the winter months, the largest ash trees were felled and the trunks were split and corded. A large fire was lighted at night, and soon a steamboat called to purchase the wood; from the store of goods carried by the vessel, needed articles were purchased.

By the end of the first year, the family had substantial food and suitable clothing and were better prepared to cope with fever. As others were doing, the men of the family felled the towering cypresses and transported them to the banks of the rivers. Rafts of cypress logs were loaded with cordwood, and at high water the trip downstream to New Orleans was made. With the proceeds from the sale of cypress and cordwood, family supplies were obtained.

Each successive year the savings of the family increased. Their livestock—cattle, hogs, and horses—grew in number, as did their cultivated acreage. Eventually they purchased the lands they had farmed for years. Inevitably, around the first settlement a village appeared.

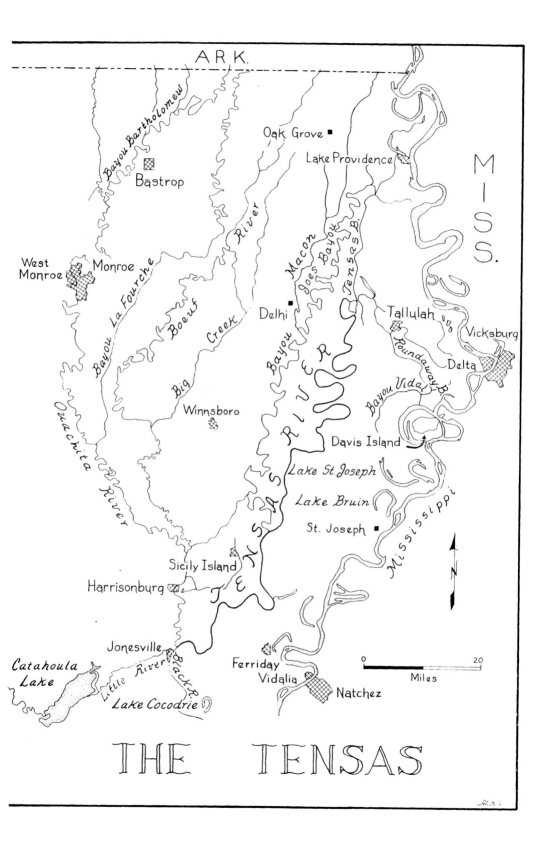

Another more affluent type of pioneer, the planter with his slaves, abandoned the worn-out lands in the South Atlantic States and moved into the basin. During the years 1830-1850, the richest cotton lands of the world were brought into cultivation along the banks of Bayou Macon, Roundaway Bayou, Vidal Bayou, Joes Bayou, the Tensas River, and other watercourses. Plantations were located on the crests of natural levees; these lands were higher, better drained, less subject to overflow, less difficult to clear, and easier to cultivate. Also, the natural levees bordering navigable streams enabled planters to have their own boat landings.

By 1850, a ribbon of plantations had been established along the navigable streams. Each planter built levees to protect his lands from floods. Not until the passage of the Swamp Land Act of 1850 were levee districts formed and a unified levee system established. Even then the danger from floods, though diminished, did not cease. Occasionally a crevasse in the Mississippi levees resulted in a tremendous volume of water pouring down Bayou Macon and the Tensas River, flooding the entire basin. The destruction of dykes in Arkansas during the Civil War brought annual spring floods to Bayou Macon.

The decade ending in 1860 was the golden age of the basin. Great plantations with scores of slaves grew large crops of cotton, which were sent down Bayou Macon and the Tensas on steamboats to New Orleans. David Hun in 1860 owned 1,700 slaves and a dozen or more plantations. The Morgan family were also great owners of lands and slaves. Perhaps the greatest of all, certainly in the dimensions of his dreams, was Norman Frisby, who became a legend in the basin.

Frisby acquired 42,000 acres of land with a frontage of 25 miles on the Tensas River. He dreamed of making his private domain independent, protected by a chain of levees. He planned ultimately to grow 10,000 bales of cotton annually and produce enough food and livestock for his army of slaves. He hoped also to build the most fabulous mansion in the South. On the eve of the Civil War, construction of Frisby's dream mansion got under way. Bricks made by his slaves were too soft, and imported ones from New Orleans were used.

After planting his second crop of cotton, Frisby bought the largest cotton gin available at New Orleans. When the boat bringing the gin up the Tensas stalled because of low water, the gin machinery was transferred to a barge and the engine attached to a paddle wheel to provide the needed power. The cotton gin literally churned up the river.

The Civil War came; and, with the approach of Federal troops, many of Frisby's slaves ran away. The planter employed severe means to prevent their departure. In addition he attempted to divert the river from its normal course as a means of surrounding his plantation with water and impenetrable forests. Here the war would not touch him. Realizing time would not en-able him to complete his grandiose project, Frisby fled to Texas with the remaining slaves.

After the war, bankrupt, with vitality and ambition gone, Frisby returned to his Tensas plantation. A few years later at Flowers Landing he was killed by his brother-in-law in a violent argument over a mule. A legend still persists along the Tensas to the effect that, when Frisby left for Texas, he buried kegs of gold and silver and killed the Negro slaves who assisted him in concealing the treasure. Today, all that remains of Frisby's dream plantation is a large chimney surrounded by a jungle. His thousands of acres of cotton land have returned to hardwood forests, and the land is owned by a lumber company.

Waterways and the steamboat made possible the transformation of a wilderness into rich cotton plantations. Early means of travel on the streams of the basin were by rafts, flatboats, and keelboats. Flatboats carried every conceivable kind of freight from the basin to New Orleans. There the cargo was sold, the boat broken up, and sold as timber. The keelboat, long and narrow, with a small cabin in the center, from sixty feet to seventy feet in length, cut the water like a knife. Before the advent of steamboats, most of the freight brought to planters on the Tensas and Bayou Macon came in keelboats.

Henry Miller Shreve in 1816 designed a shallow-draft steamboat by raising the engine from the hold of the boat to its upper deck. The first steamboat ascended the Tensas in 1837. These early steamboats were prone to accidents of collision, explosion of engine boilers, and sinkings from holes torn in the bottom by snags. Eventually the stern-wheeler and a better system of maintaining boiler pressure reduced accidents and loss of life.

Except in time of high water, the largest steamboats were unable to travel on the streams of the basin. Boats with a carrying capacity of 800 to 1,000 bales of cotton came up the Tensas 160 miles to Guyers Bayou in perfect safety. More than sixty miles of Bayou Macon was navigable. Boats also navigated Joes Bayou, Roundaway Bayou, Vidal Bayou, and other watercourses. Richmond and later Tallulah were served by steamboats. One observer noted that steamers were plowing up and down the forests in the long, deep watercourses of the basin, and cotton plantations were being established up to the water's edge.

Effects of the Civil War were extreme. Plantations were devastated, towns and villages destroyed. In Madison Parish only two houses were left standing, and the towns of Richmond and Delhi burned. Levees on the Mississippi, as well as Bayou Macon and the Tensas, either fell into disrepair or were washed away. The aftermath of long duration was constant flooding and abandonment of plantations and farms. Disease, starvation, and migration reduced the population.

The streams continued to be virtually the only means of transportation until the 1880's. In 1869, C. B. Cooley with his boats entered the Tensas trade, and met little competition until 1880, when the steamboats of Captains Fred and Jack Banks began to ply the waters of the area.

The Tensas-Macon was navigable from November 1 to July 1. During the year 1885, three steamboats with tonnage capacity ranging from 87 tons to 191 tons and drawing from $3\frac{1}{2}$ feet to $5\frac{1}{2}$ feet of water plied these streams. In all, sixty trips were made by the vessels, traveling 140 miles above the mouth of the Tensas River and 200 miles above the mouth of Bayou Macon. Ten years later six steamboats made a total of 96 trips, stopping at 150 freight landings.

After 1910, the importance of the Tensas-Macon as arteries of commerce and communication declined. Railroads, highways, and other means of communication supplanted water transportation; yet the two streams still play an important role in the region. Water from the two streams is used to irrigate fields of rice, cotton, and other crops. Commercial fishing—always of considerable importance—still goes on. Sportsmen from far afield drive hundreds of miles to hunt deer and other wild game in the forests bordering the streams.

The Ouachita-Black

By JOHN D. WINTERS

FROM THE FLAT RIPARIAN LANDS of eastern Arkansas and Louisiana, bordering the Mississippi, over to the red hills of the north-central part of both states, the terrain is laced with a matrix of small rivers, bayous, and creeks that meander like murky-colored snakes across the land. Eventually many of them converge, and empty their collective waters into Red River.

In this giant floodplain once dwelt the mysterious mound builders. Here, too, passed the ill-starred Hernando de Soto and René Robert Cavelier, Sieur de la Salle, the young Jean Baptiste Le Moyne, Sieur de Bienville, and the enigmatic Felipe Enrique Neri, Baron de Bastrop, possessed by dreams of empire, followed by a steady trickle of Anglo-Saxon homeseekers refugeeing from the worn lands of Georgia and the Carolinas. During the Civil War, the woods echoed to the sound of marching armies, jayhawkers, guerrillas, traitors, and patriots. Reconstruction brought with it carpetbaggers, scalawags, defeated but still-defiant Southerners, and a number of famous outlaws. Jesse James and the Younger brothers trod the same ground and crossed the same rivers as had James Bowie, Louis Antoine Juchereau de Saint-Denis, and other heroes of an earlier day. Many left a name to perpetuate an experience.

West of the Mississippi are three main rivers: the Boeuf, the Ouachita, and the Black. Boeuf River rises in southeastern Arkansas and flows in a southwesterly direction into Louisiana. Between the small towns of Oak Ridge and Epps the river is joined by Bonne Idee Bayou. After proceeding only a short distance, the two streams separate. The left fork becomes Bayou Lafourche, which, after wandering to the southwest and creating a huge swamp east of Monroe, rejoins the Boeuf some thirty miles below. On the east, Boeuf River is followed and joined by Big Creek, near Liddieville. Southward, the Boeuf is fattened by the sluggish waters of Deer Creek, an arm of Bayou Macon.

To the west and paralleling the Boeuf is the larger, wider, more beautiful Ouachita, which crosses the border into Louisiana from Arkansas some thirty miles north of Monroe. Bayou Bartholomew is the first important stream which unites with the Ouachita on the east. This bayou also loops its tortuous way down from Arkansas. West of the river, Bayou de l'Outre winds out of the pine-clad hills and discharges into the Ouachita. Near Monroe, Bayou D'Arbonne—fed by man-made lakes Corney, D'Arbonne and Claiborne, and by numerous small bayous and streams—joins the river.

Many miles below, on the east side near Sicily Island, Boeuf River, now much enlarged, flows into the Ouachita. Black River, formed by the wandering Bayou Macon and the Tensas River, makes confluence with the Ouachita and with Little River from the west at Jonesville. At this juncture the Ouachita loses its identity and becomes Black River. As the Black coils southward to empty into Red River, it is joined by several short creeks and bayous.

In prehistoric times the Boeuf and Ouachita valleys were huge channels through which swollen rivers, unfettered by man, emptied much of their surplus waters. Broad but shallow rivers were easily etched into the soft alluvial soil by waters rushing toward the sea. Floodwater filled and drowned these interior streams, inundating the land. After the floods had subsided, dark cypress swamps, occasional elevated deltas, and impenetrable canebrakes were left behind. Sodden, low-lying lands, shrouded with cypress, never dried out.

Into this primordial wilderness came the first settlers, the Indians. Here on the higher ground along the banks of the streams, upon built-up deltas, or upon giant man-made earth mounds they built their round or square houses of wood, grass, and mud. Because game and fish abounded, the aborigines labored less arduously for food. Here and there short foot trails traversed a part of the area, but it was the web of streams that furnished the Indian his chief transportation and communication systems.

These mound builders, without the benefit of modern machinery, constructed gigantic elevations above the floodplains. The purpose of these mounds was threefold: for habitation and protection during periods of flood, for government and religious ceremonials, and for burials. Mounds are found throughout the area, along the Ouachita, Macon, Tensas, Black, and Little rivers, Catahoula Lake, and Bayou Bartholomew. Many of these have escaped the ravages of modern progress and are objects of intense study and speculation. Here archaeologists are still unearthing pottery of unusual design, symmetry, and coloration, and arrowheads, weapons, and large bones of prehistoric men.

The first white man to visit this watery heartland of Louisiana was probably Hernando de Soto. Embittered by his long and fruitless search for the fabled gold and riches of North America, De Soto, with his hungry and demoralized remnant of an army, moved southward in the spring of 1542 along the waters of the lovely Anilco River in search of an escape route from the hostile wilderness to the civilized refuge of Mexico.

Attempts had been made to use the western banks of the Mississippi as a route of march, but impassable swamps had diverted De Soto to the Anilco some fifty miles to the west. The Anilco, according to some recent cartographers and historians, was the Ouachita.

The dispirited Spaniards pushed southward, stopping briefly to pillage small Indian villages. Eventually the wanderers approached the large town of Anilco, headquarters for the tribal ruler. According to reports left by two of De Soto's men, Anilco, probably the present town of Jonesville, had some four hundred houses clustered about a beautiful central square. On a high mound which overlooked the settlement was the palace of the Anilco ruler. De Soto found the proud chieftain ready to defend his capital with more than a thousand warriors. The Spaniards attacked, and the Indians fled to one of the many towns that could be seen in the distance. De Soto set up camp on the high mound to give his bone-weary men a rest.

Days later a small party of Anilcos arrived at the camp, bearing a cloak of feathers and a necklace of pearls as a peace offering. De Soto presented a few trinkets to the natives, who as they departed promised that their people would soon return with other gifts. While the greedy Spaniards waited, they looted the deserted city and nearby towns, taking rich stores of maize, walnuts, beans, and dried persimmons. The Anilcos failed to return.

De Soto later crossed the swamps over to the Mississippi River and visited a more friendly tribe, the Guachoyas, on Lake St. Joseph. An alliance was signed with them against Anilco. The Spaniards and Guachoyas attacked, and the Anilcos were defeated. Many Indians were murdered; their heads were mounted on poles in the public square. During the summer of 1542, De Soto again marched his men through the wilderness to Guachoya. Long wracked by fever, De Soto died soon afterward. His body was buried in a hollow, weighted log in the Mississippi to prevent possible molestation by unfriendly Indians. Luis de Moscoso, who assumed leadership of the depleted band, finally succeeded in building boats and set out with the survivors down the Mississippi to the Gulf of Mexico. Spain made no attempt to colonize this area, since no great riches had been found.

Nearly a century and a half later, La Salle, in making his historic trip down the Mississippi for France, stopped briefly among the Tensas Indians, who then inhabited the eastern perimeter of the Tensas River Basin. The Anilcos and earlier Indian tribes had disappeared, and the Natchezan, Caddoan, and Tunica linguistic groups had taken their place.

In 1703, a temporary mission was established along the Ouachita by

Bienville and Saint-Denis near the present site of Monroe. Some twelve years later Antoine Crozat ordered that a trading post be built on the same spot. The impoverished and isolated post was also deserted after several years. From time to time French fur traders entered the Ouachita region, but did not attempt to make a permanent settlement.

The next people to move into the area were the Natchez Indians. They were driven from Natchez in 1730 after they attempted to exterminate the French settlers at Fort Rosalie. In Catahoula, near Sicily Island, the small French force commanded by Saint-Denis attacked with cannon and musket and slaughtered them. With this disastrous defeat, the Natchez Indians ceased to exist as a tribe.

Eventually a few French settlers with their Negro slaves drifted into the Ouachita Valley and settled. Most were hunters and trappers, and none earned their living from agriculture. No organized communities had been established by 1762, when France secretly transferred Louisiana back to Spain. After this change in ownership, a few Spaniards moved into the territory. However, it was not until 1782 that the Spanish undertook the organization of the Ouachita country. In that year Governor Esteban Miró assigned Don Juan Filhiol the task of establishing a military and trading post on the Ouachita. In 1785, this post was located at the present site of Monroe; and five years later Fort Miró was erected to protect the inhabitants of the area from hostile Indian attacks and to drive out all English and American squatters.

Two royalist refugees, Joseph, Marquis de Maison Rouge, from France, and Prussian-born Felipe Enrique Neri, Baron de Bastrop, arrived in Spanish Louisiana in 1795 seeking political asylum. Contracts with these two gentlemen were signed by Governor Francisco Luis Hector de Noyelles, Baron de Carondelet. Maison Rouge received three huge tracts of land along the Ouachita, and Bastrop was granted two million acres to the east, in what is now Morehouse and West Carroll parishes, for colonization.

Maison Rouge brought in a few settlers, but his inclusion of Americans angered the Spanish officials. His despotic business tactics caused trouble with his colonists.

In 1797, Bastrop settled 99 people on his land, a figure far short of the 500 families he had agreed to bring. The Baron built a sawmill and trading post and devised a scheme for cultivating wheat and milling flour. The plan did not succeed.

Baron de Bastrop never received royal confirmation of his grant; when Louisiana was transferred to the United States in 1803, the claim was brought into new focus. Through complicated swapping, mortgaging, selling, and lawsuits the baron finally surrendered his last lien on the property; and the huge domain was acquired by two astute speculators, Abraham Morhouse

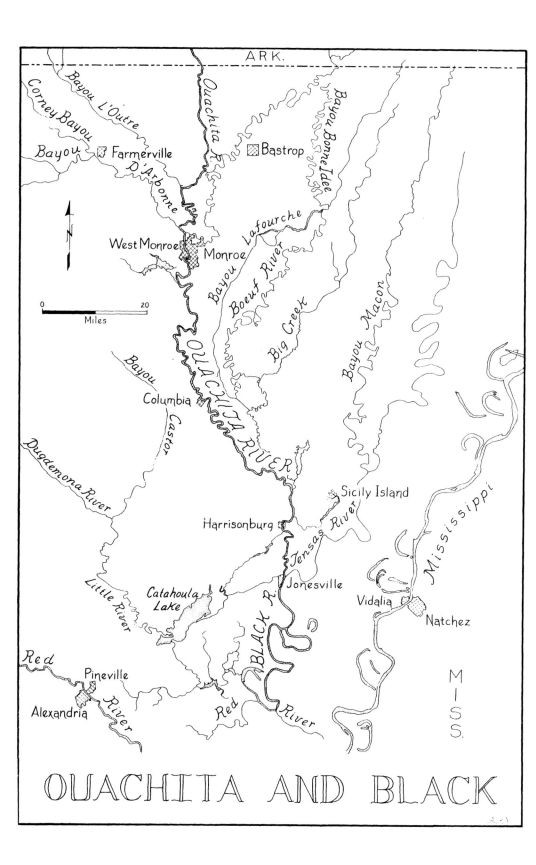

(the original spelling of the family name) and Charles Lynch. Soon afterward, Bastrop left to settle in Texas.

The maze of rivers and bayous served the white men as the initial means of entry into upper Louisiana. Boats of various shapes and sizes, propelled by paddle and pole and sometimes by sail, were used. Most freight was floated downstream on flatboats to New Orleans. The return upstream was a long and arduous undertaking. To avoid treacherous currents the boats hugged the banks and often had to zigzag from shore to shore to avoid changing currents.

It was not until Henry Miller Shreve designed a light-draft steamboat with deck-mounted machinery to drive side-wheels that the shallow, narrow interior waterways could be negotiated by steam-powered boats. In the spring of 1819 such a boat, the *James Monroe*, entered the Ouachita and traveled as far north as Fort Miró. The citizens celebrated the occasion by renaming their little town Monroe.

Steamboating was beset with dangers. There were many tragic accidents along the Ouachita and its tributaries. Steamboats sometimes collided; disastrous fires raced through their wooden structures; shallow keels sometimes struck hidden snags and sank, drowning many aboard; and fragile, overheated boilers blew up, scalding, killing, and maiming both crew and passengers. Groundings on submerged bars added to the discomfort and expense of river travel.

In the early days of steamboating on inland waters, the arrival of a boat was an occasion of enjoyment and celebration. Long, repeated blasts from the powerful boat whistle, sometimes accompanied by the firing of a cannon, heralded the approaching boat. People gathered to buy newspapers and magazines, to eat fresh oysters in season, and to enjoy the fine liquors and wines provided by the bartender. At times dances were held in the main cabin of the larger boats. Frequent fights enlivened the occasion.

Steam traffic gradually increased. From November to July boats could easily proceed as far north as Monroe, and during high water could steam to Arkadelphia, Arkansas. During the dry season steamers could go only as far as Harrisonburg.

Within the Ouachita-Boeuf system, 1,500 miles were navigable. Extensive clearing of timbers and logs and the digging of short canals or cutoffs to eliminate miles of meanderings opened up most of the Boeuf, Macon, Tensas, and many other waterways much of the year.

Some of the streams were enclosed in levees and deepened. In 1852, State engineers suggested that a series of locks be constructed from Harrisonburg northward into Arkansas to make the Ouachita navigable at all seasons. However, it was not until the second decade of the twentieth century that the Federal Government carried out this proposal.

The Civil War radically altered the lives of the people of northeast Louisiana and sorely disrupted river transportation. The Confederate outlets into Red River, and from that river into the Mississippi, were largely sealed off by Federal gunboats by 1863. Periodically, naval vessels entered the Black, the Ouachita, and other tributaries and destroyed or captured Confederate property, bringing a taste of the shooting war to the Ouachita-Boeuf basins.

Several battles and numerous skirmishes between opposing forces took place along the Mississippi, but the interior served more as a recruiting and training area and as a granary than as a battlefield. Minor engagements did take place at Oak Ridge, Monroe, and Harrisonburg, and in West Carroll Parish, in Richland Parish, and in the central sections of Madison and upper Morehouse parishes.

Gunboat activity on the Ouachita began in May, 1863. Commander S. E. Woodworth with four enemy gunboats entered Black River from the Red under orders to capture two Confederate ships, the *Webb* and the *Queen of the West*. His forward progress was halted at Fort Beauregard on the heights of Harrisonburg. After two days of ineffectual bombardment of the fort, Woodworth retired to Red River, having failed to capture the Confederate boats but having succeeded in destroying huge stores of sugar, molasses, rum, salt, and bacon.

Sporadically other Federal gunboats entered the area. At Trinity, a Union squadron successfully destroyed a cache of ammunition and seized several small steamers. Along the Tensas, Little, and Ouachita rivers, the Union navy destroyed ferries, warehouses, cotton gins, and boats. In their greedy search for cotton, Union commanders ranged wide and deep throughout north Louisiana.

With the end of the war came a revival of river shipping. Several new packet companies were organized in St. Louis. Faster, bigger, and more palatial boats were provided and regular sailing schedules were maintained. Annually the Ouachita region shipped more than 150,000 bales of cotton to St. Louis and New Orleans. St. Louis gradually began to replace New Orleans as a main market. Some of the steamboats on the Ouachita could haul several thousand bales of cotton. The peak of water traffic was reached in the 1880's, but as the railroad began to inch into the area, the slower river freight began to decline.

The development of land transportation in the Ouachita-Boeuf valleys lagged far behind water transportation. All roads and trails in the area, until well after the Civil War, existed primarily as connecting links between rural settlements and river ports. Huge teams of oxen brought cotton and other produce over deeply rutted dirt roads from inland areas. During the rainy season these few roads became quagmires difficult for wagons to travel.

Unbridged streams swollen with floodwaters were both difficult and dangerous to ford.

The first major road in the area ran along the northern perimeter from Lake Providence on the Mississippi over to Prairie Mer Rouge, to the highlands of Bastrop, thence to Monroe. Hand-operated ferries crossed the various streams. Early settlers sometimes entered the region via this route. During the dry season travelers often used this road to the Mississippi, where they could catch a steamboat.

Around 1800, a road from Harrisonburg to Vidalia was laid out and later extended to Alexandria. A stagecoach began operating over this route in 1849. Another little-traveled trail was blazed in 1810 between Sicily Island and Rodney, on the Mississippi. It was not until 1838 that the area between Monroe and Vicksburg was surveyed, and a horse trail was hacked through the endless canebrake of the Tensas and Lafourche swamps. An irregular stagecoach service was opened to Vicksburg in 1850. During the rainy season these routes were impassable. It was not until after the Civil War that necessary earth embankments, bridges, levees, and plank roads were built to give the area an all-weather highway.

A railroad between Vicksburg and Monroe was begun in 1855, and the first train began operations in 1860. War disrupted the rail service, for Union raiding parties burned bridges, ripped up rails, and destroyed depots. Service was not resumed until 1870. A railroad bridge across the Ouachita was completed in 1882; by 1884, trains could travel all the way to Shreveport.

Before the coming of the railroad, population growth remained steady but small. The rich delta lands accessible by river or bayou were the first to be settled. Wagon roads and railroads helped to stimulate more rapid settlement of inland areas.

The majority of the people who came were of Anglo-Saxon stock who had pushed westward from Georgia, Alabama, the Carolinas, Virginia, and Tennessee. Few remnants of the earlier French and Spanish culture, except place names, remained. Small, new towns and farm communities began to rise. By 1860, in the ten choice agricultural parishes, the slave population outnumbered the whites, while the six more isolated and hilly parishes remained predominantly white.

During the war the population was much disrupted by lawless jayhawkers, Union raiders, and Confederate forces. Many people fled westward to protect their slave property. Reconstruction brought alien carpetbag rule and in its wake "protectors" of southern rights such as Frank and Jesse James, the Younger boys, and others. The Knights of the White Camelia also traveled the country roads and retaliated against carpetbag atrocities.

Eventually, the purely rural aspects of the region began to change.

Highways, railroads, the discovery of gas and oil, the presence of virgin timbers, good weather conditions, and the availability of a plentiful supply of water helped to entice industry. Kraft paper mills, huge lumber mills, plywood factories, chemical and carbon plants, refineries, and allied industries moved in and are continuing to come in today.

Because of two world wars, agriculture became more and more mechanized. Cotton, long the one money crop of the region, gave ground to soybeans, peas, trees, and cattle. Mechanization developed as labor costs increased and rural populations declined. According to the 1960 census, in the sixteen parishes making up the Ouachita-Boeuf region, ten showed a decrease in population in the past ten years. Six parishes, where large industries and gas and oil fields were developed, showed population increases. Racial figures have drastically changed, and in only three parishes do the Negroes outnumber the whites.

Today, man-made levees and canals have channeled and controlled the floodwaters; huge pumps and deep ditches have reduced the size of swamps and dried out much of the land. Giant bulldozers have cleared and turned the unused areas into highly productive cotton, corn, bean, and cattle lands. Gas and oil, in increasing supply, are being discovered. Private lumber companies and State and Federal conservation agencies maintain huge timber preserves that guard the future of the lumber industry. These forest reserves teem with wild game and add greatly to the natural beauty. On the rivers, occasionally the dull throb of a diesel-powered tug pushing a long line of barges competes with the high-pitched whine of the pleasure craft. Ever increasing industry continues to tap the plentiful waters for cooling, dissolving, powering, and flushing purposes, and growing municipalities draw heavily upon the streams.

Most of these rivers and bayous still retain much of their wild beauty and help to make the Ouachita-Boeuf area a truly beautiful land.

The Upper Mississippi

Louisiana Department of Agriculture

Harriet Magruder, A History of Louisiana

De Soto Discovering the Mississippi

An old print

Keelboat on the Mississippi

An old print

Flatboat at Bayou Sara

An old print

Interior of Flatboat

Levee Repair Along the Mississippi

United States Army Corps of Engineers

Laying Concrete Mats, Mississippi River Levee

United States Army Corps of Engineers

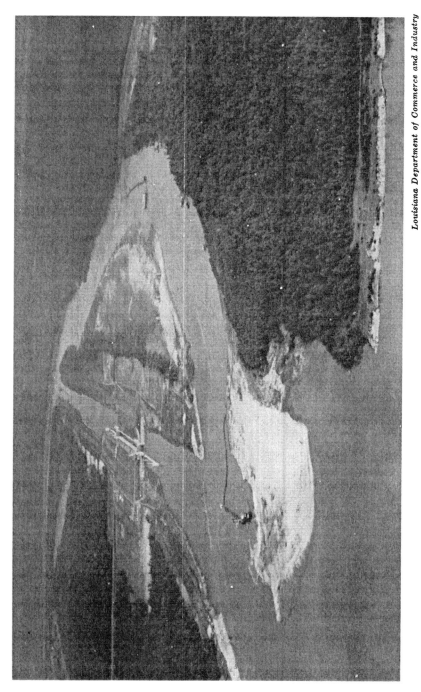

The Old River Project

Louisiana Department of Commerce and Industry

Louisiana Department of Commerce and Industry

The Old River Lock

United States Army Corps of Engineers

30-Barge Tow on the Mississippi

Edwin Adams Davis

Headwaters of the Tensas

Edwin Adams Davis

The Tensas

Confluence of the Ouachita, Tensas, and Little Rivers

Town of Jonesville

Convergence of the Ouachita and Boeuf Rivers

E. E. Johnson, Harrisonburg, La.

Old Duty Ferry on the Ouachita River

E. E. Johnson, Harrisonburg, La.

Part II | *Northwest Louisiana*

Bayou Dorcheat

By MARIETTA M. LeBRETON

RISING IN NEVADA COUNTY, Arkansas, Bayou Dorcheat flows in a southerly direction 122 miles through Arkansas and Louisiana. It enters Lake Bistineau, which joins Loggy Bayou, to form a continuous passage from Arkansas to the Red River of Louisiana. Lake Bistineau is a long, narrow body of water consisting presently of a surface area of 20,000 acres lying in three parishes of Louisiana. The lake is fed by Dorcheat, Clark's Bayou, and numerous other smaller streams. The drainage area of the Dorcheat is approximately 1,400 square miles and is composed of fertile farmland, timberland, and swampland. While many residents of Louisiana may never have heard of this small stream, Bayou Dorcheat has left its imprint on the history of the northwestern part of the State.

In the early history Bayou Dorcheat, like many of the other numerous streams of Louisiana, played an important role in peopling the State. Because of the need for easy accessibility to water transportation, the early settlers usually inhabited, when possible, lands adjacent to navigable streams. The rivers and bayous of Louisiana became the lifelines of many nascent communities. Bayou Dorcheat was accessible from the Red and Mississippi rivers and navigable as far as present-day Minden three to six months of the year, making it attractive to both Indian and white settlers. The lands along the banks of the bayou were part of the region claimed and settled by the Caddoan Confederacy of Indians who occupied eastern Texas, southern Arkansas, and northwestern Louisiana. The name "Dorcheat" itself is probably of Caddoan derivation and means "people," referring to one of the Caddoan tribes. The name "Bistineau" is believed also to have originated with the Caddos and means "big broth." The Indians evidently so named the lake because of the large amounts of froth which they observed floating on its surface at certain times. In 1835, the Caddos signed a treaty with the United States Government giving up their land claims in Louisiana and migrated out of the State.

Long before the Caddos gave up claim to the land, white settlers had begun to move into the area. Probably many of these early pioneers were traders, trappers, or hunters lingering in the Dorcheat region for only short periods of time. There seems to have been no great interest in the stream until the early nineteenth century, when references to Bayou Dorcheat began to appear in travel accounts and in works describing Louisiana. In 1805, Dr. John Sibley, the Indian Agent at Natchitoches, mentioned the "Daichet" in his account of Louisiana. Eleven years later, William Darby noted that until that time the "Dacheet" and other streams of the area were unknown and had never been described in any work on Louisiana. He wrote that "the Dacheet [sic] in particular contains the most extensive range of rich soil to be found in the Northwestern angle of the state of Louisiana." Darby also presented a detailed, favorable description of Lake Bistineau.

By the second decade of the nineteenth century settlement began along the waterway. The Dorcheat was not invaded by glory seekers, adventurers, or those interested in obtaining easy wealth. Its appeal was limited to the hardy yeoman stock of pioneers who were seeking good, fertile soil in which to implant their roots. The early settlers of the bayou were typical, self-reliant, independent, small farmers who made their way up Loggy Bayou, Lake Bistineau, and Bayou Dorcheat because navigation of the Red River was blocked by logjams. Some of the early pioneers simply used these waterways as a route to a new home in the interior; others lingered on the banks of the streams temporarily; and still others settled in the Dorcheat region permanently.

One of the first permanent white settlers of the Dorcheat was Issac Alden, who migrated from New Orleans in 1811 and occupied a site approximately eight miles east of the present city of Minden. The next notable white inhabitant was John Murrell, who left Tennessee in the winter of 1818 with his family and belongings in search of a new home in the West. The Murrells floated down the Cumberland River to Nashville, where they joined other immigrants trekking westward. The group made their way down the Cumberland, Ohio, and Mississippi rivers to the mouth of the Red River. Ascending this stream, they proceeded to Long Prairie, Arkansas, from which John Murrell moved his family to a vacant cabin in the Flat Lick area. In 1821, Newt Drew moved from Black Bayou to Dorcheat, where he constructed a sawmill and a gristmill. Around Drew's mills there developed a town, Overton, which for years was the main landing point on the bayou.

Thus settlement of the Dorcheat commenced, but the history of the bayou was a precarious one. Some of the early villages and towns became permanent; others ceased to exist after a few years. But regardless of their destiny, all of these communities were affected by the waterways of Bayou Dorcheat, Lake Bistineau, and Loggy Bayou, which connected them with the Red and

Mississippi rivers and ultimately with New Orleans and other river ports. Until the railroad arrived in the late nineteenth century and Red River was opened to navigation, these watercourses formed a major artery of commerce.

Throughout the nineteenth century, when Bayou Dorcheat served as the principal means of transportation and communication for a wide area of Louisiana, her banks were lined with wharves, landing areas, and warehouses, where goods were unloaded and stored until they were distributed to the general mercantile stores in the rapidly developing area. With the beginning of the steamboat era, shipping activities on the Dorcheat increased. Farmers eagerly waited for the waters of the bayou to rise so that the steamers could bring them supplies and pick up cotton for the return trip. The ships carried such uninteresting but necessary articles as sugar, meat, flour, furniture, and agricultural implements to the settlers, and for the return trip loaded up with cotton, the principal crop of the area, usually destined for New Orleans.

The steamboat age on Bayou Dorcheat spawned many interesting and exciting tales and stories. It is said that one of the early steamboats on the bayou, after discharging its cargo and loading up with cotton, began its return trip to the Red River. After entering Lake Bistineau, the steamer caught fire and burned to the water's edge. A frantic woman passenger was seen leaping from the burning vessel with a child under each arm. Fortunately, she and one of the children were rescued by a nearby observer of the tragic scene. Misfortune also befell another steamboat, the *Shamrock*, which after many successful trips burned on the Dorcheat in 1850 with the loss of one life.

The list of steamboats which plied the Dorcheat was long and included both side-wheelers and stern-wheelers. Many of them only served as cargo carriers.

Of a more exciting nature were the steamers which served as passenger ships as well as cargo vessels. Among these were ships with such stirring names as the *Danube*, the *Jewel*, and the *Maria Louise*. Many and gay were the entertainments provided for the passengers aboard these packets, as is evidenced by a letter printed in the Minden *Webster Tribune*, February 8, 1883. The letter, written on the steamboat *Alexandria*, at the mouth of Loggy Bayou on February 1, 1883, gave the following description of a trip: ". . .We had fifteen passengers aboard, and had quite a pleasant time coming down the lake and bayou. We arrived at the mouth of Loggy bayou late Wednesday evening, and there tied up for the night. . . . We leave for New Orleans this evening on the Danbue. She has quite a large crowd of young ladies and gentlemen. The Long Springs band is on board and will furnish music for us on our way down." Clearly the writer had enjoyed his

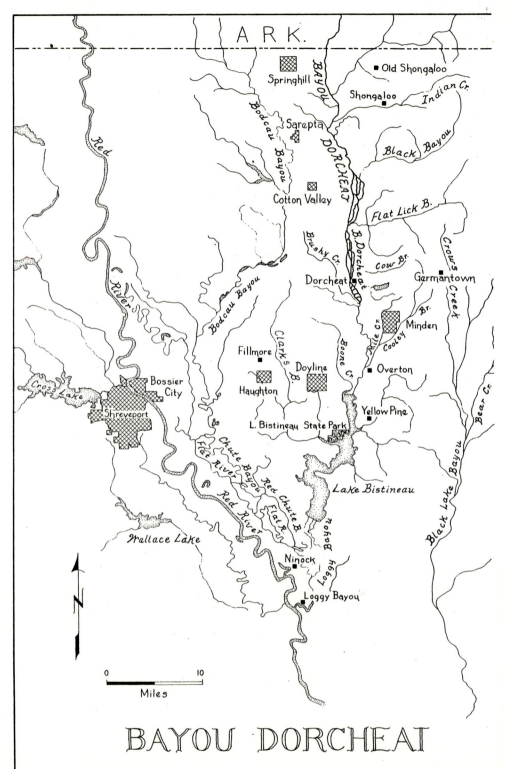

BAYOU DORCHEAT

adventure on Bayou Dorcheat and Lake Bistineau and was looking forward to the rest of the journey.

Navigation of Bayou Dorcheat gradually led to the establishment of many interesting and some unique villages and towns. Of these, Overton was one of the earliest and most important. The town grew up around Newt Drew's mills, eventually becoming the major cotton port for farmers on Bayou Dorcheat. In the decades of the 1820's and 1830's, Overton enjoyed a tremendous growth, so that in 1836 it was named the seat of government for Claiborne Parish. However, the bayou town was soon overshadowed by its larger neighbor, Minden, which had been founded in 1835 approximately three miles to the east. Overton's development was hindered also by its extremely unhealthy location. The town was periodically ravaged by epidemics, especially one in 1839 which, according to legend, claimed three hundred lives. Gradually Overton was abandoned, so that by the time of the Civil War it was almost a deserted area. A quarter of a century later, a cotton field covered the site, and today only a cemetery on a hill marks the location of the once thriving bayou port.

With the decline of Overton, Minden became the most important town in the Dorcheat region. The site of the present city was purchased in 1835 by Charles L. Veeder, who wanted to construct an inn for travelers on the old Military Road. The next year, Veeder laid out Minden, named it for his hometown in Germany, and attempted to have it declared the seat of government for Claiborne Parish; but the competition of Newt Drew and Overton was too great. Evidently Veeder felt that having the parish seat established in his town would contribute to its growth and certainly to a rise in the value of real estate.

Undampened by his failure, he began a promotion campaign to attract businessmen and investors to Minden, and in 1838 he obtained authorization from the State to establish an academy called the Minden Academy. In 1850, the academy was reorganized as a girls' school and finally in 1854 rechartered as the Minden Female College, which some people claim is the oldest college in North Louisiana. Minden was incorporated in 1850 and became the governmental center of newly created Webster Parish in 1871. Because the town was served by railroads and roads, it continued to enjoy a prominent position culturally and commercially even after Bayou Dorcheat ceased to be the main artery of commerce.

Eight miles east of Minden there developed the most interesting of all the communities along the Dorcheat. This was Germantown, sometimes called Dutchtown, founded by the disciples of the mystic Bernhard Muller, Count Leon. After his banishment from Germany in 1830 for alleged participation in revolutionary activities and for teaching unorthodox religious views, the count led his followers across the Atlantic to Pennsylvania, where they joined George Rapp's colony. Friction and trouble soon developed between the two leaders, so the count and his disciples decided to move on and establish their own community. After an unsuccessful colonizing attempt in Pennsylvania, the group made their way to Grand Ecore, where they landed in February, 1834. There they began a settlement, but yellow fever broke out, resulting in the death of the count and some of his followers. The survivors, led by Count Leon's wife, decided to move to higher ground, which they felt would be more healthy. Ascending Red River and Bayou Dorcheat, they established Germantown, approximately eight miles east of Minden, in 1836. The settlement operated on a communal basis, with particular functions assigned to individuals according to talent and training, and all property was held in common. The entire day of the colonists—work, worship, and recreation—was planned. They planted cotton, but held no slaves. The Germans also engaged in handicrafts and commerce. The colony began to decline in number of settlers until it finally failed in 1871.

In the vicinity of Loggy Bayou there developed another interesting community. This settlement was Ninock, located between the Red River and Loggy Bayou. The beginning of Ninock came when Peabody Atkinson Morse settled a grant of land in 1837. Morse, a native of Massachusetts and a relative of the inventor of the telegraph, had come to Natchitoches earlier with his brother, who was a government surveyor. There he met, fell in love with, and married the daughter of a well-known French family. The young couple moved to the Ninock grant, where they established their home, developing it into one of the great plantations of the Red River area.

Many of the other notable settlements of the Dorcheat were dependent on natural resources for their establishment. Yellow Pine was one of a group of sawmill towns established by the Long Bell Company. The town consisted of houses for the employees, a commissary, a hotel, churches, schools, and most importantly a sawmill. A railroad connected the mill with the forests in the surrounding area. As the trees were cut, the town began to decline, with the residences, hotel, and mill gradually being torn down. In Yellow Pine, farming and stock raising replaced the logging industry, but lumbering generally remained an important part of the economy of the Dorcheat region. Many other towns owed their origin to sawmills and to the extensive forests of northern Louisiana. Today, there stands a large pulp mill in Springhill which testifies to the continuing importance of the timber resources of the Dorcheat region.

The Shongaloo, Sarepta, and Cotton Valley settlements became important because of the presence of two other resources—gas and oil. The petroleum boom along the Dorcheat began with the discovery of gas and oil in the Shongaloo area in 1921. In that same year, gas was found at Sarepta and oil during the following year. The third and major field, Cotton Valley, which begins about nine miles north of Minden and extends along Bayou Dorcheat some five miles, first yielded gas in 1921 and oil three years later. The Cotton Valley field became one of the largest gas producers in the State, making Webster Parish one of the leading gas-and-oil-producing districts of Louisiana. Without a doubt, petroleum replaced timber as the leading resource of the Dorcheat region. Today these fields are having an adverse effect on Bayou Dorcheat and Lake Bistineau, since they are adding to their pollution by discharging oil-field salt and gravel washings into the waterways.

The exciting commercial days of Bayou Dorcheat now belong to history. No longer can steamboats be seen on her waters or wharves lining her banks. Some of the bayou's most interesting communities have disappeared, but other industrial towns have appeared to take their places. The Dorcheat is now a lazy stream winding through low, hilly farmland and catering to the fishermen and sportsmen of North Louisiana.

Lake Bistineau is one of the outstanding recreational features of the State. For over a century the parish and State governments have expended money and energy in enlarging and improving Lake Bistineau, so that the lake today offers excellent fishing and hunting grounds. In 1942, a large dam and spillway were completed at the lower extremity of Bistineau to assure a constant water level. The principal function today of Bayou Dorcheat and Lake Bistineau is that of recreation, but in the annals of Louisiana history and life they will retain their place as a water highway of the past.

The Red

By WALTER M. LOWREY

WHILE THE RED RIVER of Louisiana is the only important tributary to the Mississippi below the Arkansas and is impressive in its color and beauty, it is today a "dead" river for most of man's purposes. Unique among the rivers of the nation, it was created as a major artery during recorded history, grew to thriving maturity, declined to useless but cranky old age, and now slumbers in its stabilized course, awaiting a new birth in a different body. Only momentary resurgences of vigor and violence in widely separated flood periods remind man of its remarkable past.

Some of the river's daughters, the lakes which it created, still survive. Its sons, the former river ports, either sleep like the parent or take sustenance from new sources of nurture—the rich soil of the valley, the mineral deposits, and the rails and roads which helped kill the river.

The Red River rises in the hills of northern New Mexico, flows southeast to become the boundary of Texas and Oklahoma, and then enters Arkansas for the descent into the northwest corner of Louisiana. From its entrance into the State, it flows southeast for 325 miles, fed by numerous bayous and by the Ouachita and Black rivers until it nears the Mississippi west of the Felicianas. There its waters divide between the Atchafalaya River and the Mississippi for their journey to the sea. Elaborate control structures have been completed here to prevent channel changes.

Unlike the many-named Mississippi, the Red River has a distinctive coloration that made its name universal among all who saw it. The color is particularly vivid when floodwaters pour down from its headwaters reaches, leaving a reddish silt on the bordering lowlands along most of its length. Even so, Sieur Henri de Tonti exaggerated a bit when he wrote in 1690, "They call this river the Red river, because, in fact, it deposits a sand which makes the water as red as blood." Yet, nearly three hundred years later the name is still apt.

The Red

The whole history of the river and the life which fed upon it derives from the phenomenon known as "The Great Raft." The raft was a changing, shifting mass of logs and river-borne debris which clogged the main channel of the river in Louisiana in a series of logjams, interspersed with areas of open water, for a distance of about 150 miles. Even Indian legends fail to hint at a period when it did not exist. Geologists believe that it began forming near Bayou Boeuf and that its head reached a point in the floodplain near Alexandria late in the fifteenth century.

As the older portions of the raft decayed, they disintegrated and washed out to sea, while new accumulations developed above, thus keeping its length almost constant. Like a huge, 150-mile-long snake the raft crawled up the river. From 1820 to 1872, measurements of its position showed its average rate of advance upriver was four-fifths of a mile a year, though as much as five miles of debris could be deposited during a major flood. By the time Louisiana was settled, the base of the raft had climbed to a point near Natchitoches, and before its final removal in 1873 its head reached to within three miles of the Louisiana-Arkansas state line.

While the existence of such a natural barrier hindered exploration, navigation, and development of the valley, it never entirely stopped them once the natural wealth of its reaches was discovered. There were always routes around the raft which the river created to escape its self-imposed prison—mazes of bayous, chutes, passes, and lakes which paralleled the main riverbed and which even today make the valley an extremely complex area to map. As the river shifted its course or created new logjams, it dammed the mouths of some of the streams feeding it, backed up their waters, flooded surrounding lowlands, and created a great chain of natural lakes extending from the lower part of the river into Arkansas and Texas.

Some of the lakes, now with dams rebuilt by man, still exist today. These include Caddo Lake, once much larger and a part of an artery to Jefferson, Texas; Bodcau Lake, which extends into Arkansas; Cross Lake, which supplies Shreveport with water; Lakes Bistineau and Black, still fabled fishing grounds; and lovely Cane River Lake, a former major route of the Red on which Natchitoches is located.

Other equally large lakes, such as Sodo, Ferry, Bayou Pierre, and Poston lakes, were drained when the raft was removed, and their former bottoms are now rich, cultivated fields. Only old maps and navigational charts still keep alive the names of these ghosts of the past, and cotton grows where steamers once plied.

The existence of these enormous lakes with their naturally permeable dams of logs and driftwood provided a constant source of water for the main channel even during the arid seasons. Today, with many of the reservoirs drained by the removal of the raft, the runoff is rapid and the river becomes slack, almost still, in drouth periods.

While the exploration of the Red River began early in the history of Louisiana, it was only haphazardly carried out until the territory was purchased by the United States. Sieur Tonti, faithful friend of René Robert Cavelier, Sieur de la Salle, in searching for news of La Salle's lost expedition in 1689 traveled most of its length, hoping to get information from the Caddo Indian nation whose tribes inhabited its banks.

Jean Baptiste Le Moyne, Sieur de Bienville, and Louis Antoine Juchereau de Saint-Denis in 1700 left the Iberville expedition in the Mississippi to explore the Red River and to establish friendly relations with the Caddos. Saint-Denis returned to the area in 1714 to plant the first permanent settlement on the Red at Natchitoches, where the river's best channel then lay, just below the base of the raft. The post was established to be a trading center and to secure French claims to the area against the encroachment of the Spanish from the southwest.

While the Natchitoches post succeeded in its aims, there was little growth or agricultural development along the banks of the river until the American period. Mercantilist restrictions hampered trade between the French at Natchitoches and the Spanish at Los Adaes, just a few miles to the west. Even after Spain acquired Louisiana, the province of Mexico jealously guarded from the Spanish Louisianians its right to the trade west of Natchitoches.

The Caddos, a docile, friendly nation, were few in number, lived in small, scattered tribal settlements, and were not far advanced toward civilization. They caused little trouble, were loyal to the Europeans who inhabited their ancestral lands, and produced relatively little profit for the traders who visited them. With more easily accessible lands available, few Europeans braved the treacherous raft passages to make permanent homes in a river basin which might flood them out overnight. During its first century, therefore, Natchitoches was more important as a strategic military post than as a trading center.

A second settlement on the Red established by the French was Les Rapides, founded in 1723. Its location, at the site of present-day Alexandria-Pineville, was marked by shoals of rock in a two-mile portion of the river. This dangerous and vexing navigational hazard, which has lasted until today, was uncovered by the river when it shifted its bed from an older channel during the raft period there. To get over the rapids resulting from the shoals often required lightening of cargoes at that point by even the smallest boats, and portages sometimes had to be used in times of slack water. Boatmen greeted their arrivals at the rapids with sighs of relief if the water was high enough to permit uninterrupted passage, and with groans of despair if low water forced them into a long and arduous wait.

With fertile surrounding lands for agriculture, good pine timber on the northern bank which could be floated down to New Orleans for sale, and the need for warehousing and storage in the rapids area, the post continued to grow in importance. Lower down the river, the Avoyelles plain and the sediment-enriched areas around Bayou Boeuf were early magnets for settlers, though few towns of consequence resulted before the American period.

Americans who went to the Red River Valley soon after the Louisiana Purchase, such as Dr. John Sibley, Indian Agent at Natchitoches, suggested removal of the raft to attract more settlers; and early in the American period three major developments spurred demands to tame and improve the river.

First, relations between the United States and Spain on its western frontier required maintenance of a sizable military force there, and chancy river transportation made supplying these troops difficult. Second, cotton, a bulky but immensely profitable crop, had come into its own and was found eminently suited to the valley. Third, the steamboat was proved practical on western rivers by an audacious young boatman, Captain Henry Miller Shreve, and could bring easy access to settlers far up the river if the channel could be cleared.

Military necessity rather than civil need opened the way for river improvement. The United States Army worked for the removal of snags and shoals in the lower Red and for the clearing of the great raft until Congress appropriated $25,000 to survey the project in 1828. Proponents of raft removal hoped that it would prove a panacea for all the river's ills. Freed of its clogging burden, they believed, the river would deepen its main channel with an increased current. Lakes created by the jam would drain and provide new, rich, easily accessible land for cultivation. Settlers would pour into the valley on the new steamers, and defense burdens would be eased.

But the job was an enormous and seemingly impossible one to accomplish. After the Army Engineers surveyed the raft and made some test attempts to break it up, they reported that the job would take millions of dollars and then might end in failure. Lewis Cass, Secretary of War, knowing that Captain Shreve had previously cleared snags from the Mississippi and Ohio despite similarly expressed doubts of the engineers, approached him about the raft removal. Shreve confidently offered to attempt the job, using unexpended funds appropriated for the river survey.

In the spring of 1833, Shreve took his snag boat *Archimedes*, which he had designed and built for work in the Mississippi, into the Red, past the scattered settlements and the towns of Alexandria and Natchitoches to the foot of the raft. There his crew attacked the mass of rotted timbers, driving headlong into the jam to loosen some, sawing others loose, and pulling some out with the snag boat. As the ancient jam began to give way, Shreve's boats nudged loosened timbers into the mouths of streams and bayous which fed upon the river in order to keep as much water in the main channel as possible. The increased flow then floated the excess debris down the unclogged channel.

With the river at flood stage, within two days Shreve penetrated five miles into the seemingly impenetrable mass. During the first year of his operations, Shreve cleared seventy miles of the river by removing fifty-six different sections of the raft. His crews opened the river from Loggy Bayou to well above the present site of Shreveport. Further appropriations kept Shreve's force at work in the river during high-water periods for four more years, but progress slowed as they tackled the newer, tougher portions of the raft. At last, on March 7, 1838, they reached the head of the raft, and the river for the first time in centuries ran free.

Almost in the wake of the snag boats came the steamers. Shreve himself had brought the first steamboat, his *Enterprise,* into the Red on December 14, 1814; and a considerable traffic had already developed as far as Natchitoches, which docked its first steamer in 1824. However, in much of the Red, flatboats, keelboats, and pirogues were still supreme before Shreve.

The removal of the raft wrested from Natchitoches its preeminent position as the hub of valley transportation. Emigrants for Texas and Arkansas had long used the town as a base for outfitting after arriving there by overland routes from the Natchez area or by boat on the Red. It was through Natchitoches that Stephen F. Austin led his emigrant band to Texas, followed later by Sam Houston, Davy Crockett, and Jim Bowie, for the best road west from Louisiana started here, the fabled El Camino Real.

Even before raft removal, changes in the river made Campti, twenty miles to the north, a temporarily thriving rival for the Texas trade. Then Grand Ecore, a bluff four miles east of Natchitoches, became the major port of the area in the 1830's when the newly freed river shifted its main channel there. Natchitoches was joined to Grand Ecore by a road, although some steamers continued to use Cane River until at least 1885.

As Shreve's work progressed, it became evident that a trade center much farther north than Natchitoches was needed on the Red. Coates Bluff settlement already existed on a spur of land; but, in 1835, Captain Shreve shortened the river channel by cutting a canal across the spur, isolating the town. It may have been chance that the new channel he created fronted on land owned by the Shreve Town Company in which the captain was interested and where his work crews were based. Here the town of Shreveport was incorporated in 1838. The new town was well-located to dominate the Texas traffic, for it commanded the entrance to a chain of lakes and bayous which provided good navigation as far as Jefferson, Texas, a good distribution point for all of northeast Texas.

While Shreveport and Jefferson prospered and emigrants flooded into the area, the region to the north was not so fortunate. The raft began to re-form above Shreveport in the summer of 1838, just three miles north of the point where Shreve had finished his work in March of that year. It grew to a length of twenty miles before Captain Thomas Taylor Williamson removed it in 1843. Even then, the last of the raft had not been heard. Before the close of 1843, new logjams appeared, growing up the river until 1872, flooding lowlands and making navigation difficult. Settlers upriver demanded that the raft be cleared, while inhabitants of Jefferson bitterly protested the action which would drain the water route to that town. Proponents of channel clearing won; and, in 1873, Lieutenant E. A. Woodruff made quick work of destroying this final raft by using the new explosive, nitroglycerine. Constant vigilance in removing snags and incipient jams and the closing off of all lateral waterways to force the river's outflow into one channel have since prevented any recurrence of the raft.

The wonderful advantages of a raft-free river expected by those who worked for this end never came to pass. Flooding of nearby lands did decrease and the channel deepened, but the greater channel capacity rushed the river's seasonal supply of water quickly to the sea. Without the great chain of lakes and bayous to keep it fed year-round, navigation could only be intermittent. And at the same time the channel was stabilized, the railroads penetrated the river valley, giving easy, cheap, and sure transportation to the area.

Thus the significant achievement of clearing the river virtually sealed the doom of its usefulness. It became, instead of the main artery of the valley, a menace to its people—a barrier to be crossed and a drainage ditch which became a monster during its periodic flooding. Even its waters in days of increasing water demand are used as a municipal supply by only one sizable city, Bossier City; for they are heavy with minerals and salts difficult to remove. For this reason, too, many agriculturalists shun their use for irrigation.

Even at its best, navigation of the Red River was dangerous, tiresome, and expensive. United States Army Engineers reported in 1901, long after river use had virtually ceased, that over a hundred steamboat wrecks lay in the main channel between Fulton, Arkansas, and the mouth of the river. Untold numbers littered the former routes around the raft.

Besides the usual steamboat hazards of explosions, fire, and collisions with driftwood, boats in the Red faced some unique dangers. Adventurous captains often would attempt to break through newly formed portions of the raft only to be trapped and have their boats crushed. The narrow

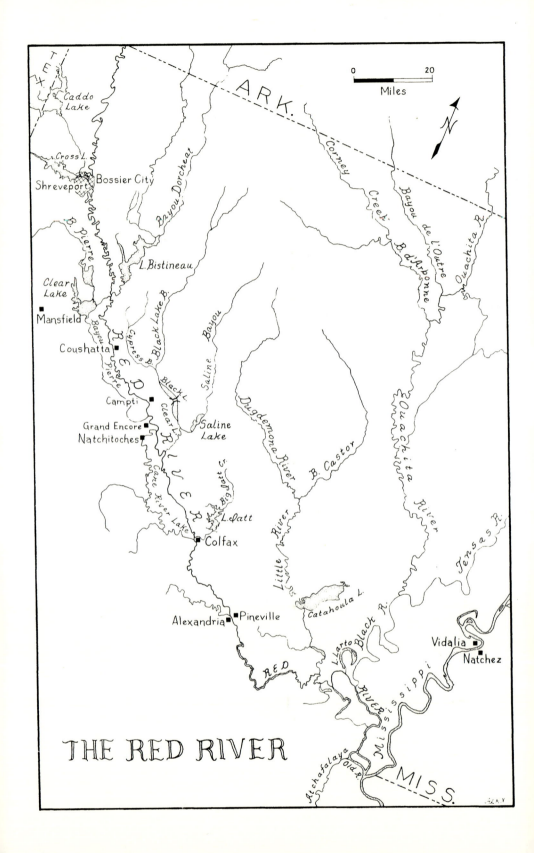

chutes and passes used by the steamers to reach off-river customers were infested with submerged stumps, dead trees which might fall at the touch of a boat, and overhanging branches which could rip away a boat's superstructure.

Shipping arrangements were peculiarly uncertain. Carriers accepted cargo to and from the raft area with reservations, and time schedules were seldom kept. Delays at the rapids were common. Frederick Law Olmstead, on a journey to the southwest, told of two Red River steamers scheduled for a Sunday departure from New Orleans. He booked passage on one which finally left the following Thursday, while the other departed a week late. His boat engaged in a dangerous race with another steamer in the narrow river channel, to the dismay of Olmstead. The boat was infested with the usual river riffraff and gamblers, the journey seemed interminable, and he was forced to share a bunk with a dangerous-looking fellow who carried a knife larger than Olmstead's.

Docking areas along newly formed routes were usually temporary structures which had to be extended far into the lakes from the gently sloping shore and were reached over "bottomless roads" impassable for much of the year. Insurance rates for cargoes were higher than those on most Mississippi River tributaries except the Arkansas, and they rose precipitously for trips above Shreveport.

In the late summer and fall, when the river was lowest, crews faced long, hot struggles to pull over sandbars, unloading freight to lighten the boat over shoals, and extricating boats from hidden snags and stumps. For the passengers the journey was tedious and uncomfortable, as few of the Red River boats reached the "floating palace" stage of comfort common on Mississippi River queens.

Despite the navigational difficulties, the riches of the valley did reach their major market in New Orleans. Cotton was the major cargo hauled by steamer on the Red, but hides, corn, and sugar also produced cargo revenue of sizable proportions. Before the Civil War, steamers were regularly taking over 250,000 bales of cotton yearly from the valley to New Orleans.

The Civil War halted the almost geometric growth of Red River commerce, although until the fall of Vicksburg and Port Hudson in 1863 the river area continued to supply the eastern Confederacy with grain and with much-needed war articles imported from Mexico through Texas.

To check the influence of the French in Mexico and to eliminate Confederate power in the Trans-Mississippi region, the Union mounted a major expedition up the Red in the spring of 1864. General Nathaniel P. Banks commanded the army of about 25,000, while Admiral David Porter was in charge of a formidable fleet of ironclads, gunboats, and transports which made a parallel advance up the river. Shreveport, the Confederate capital of the State, was the immediate objective, and the fort which defended it from river attack was armed primarily with fake cannon to fool the enemy. If the ironclads could get to Shreveport, the city would surely fall.

The river was low, however, and the largest of the gunboats had to be left below the rapids. As the still-sizable fleet which got across tried to keep pace with the army on shore a few miles away, the Confederates peppered the boats with heavy sniper fire as obstructions in the unnaturally low river delayed the advance. A curious running battle between infantry and gunboats continued while the Union army advanced almost unmolested. The Confederates under General Richard Taylor massed sufficient forces at Mansfield on April 8, 1864, to send the Union force in retreat southward. After the Battle of Pleasant Hill on the following day, Banks decided to abandon his campaign and disengage from the Confederates. The fleet, too, started downriver.

Instead of rising as it usually did in the spring, the Red continued to fall, and the retreating fleet was trapped by the rapids. The slow advance of the Confederates allowed Lieutenant Colonel Joseph Bailey and the army enough time to construct wing dams of logs and stone at the rapids to force the current into a narrow channel which floated the fleet across to safety. Remnants of these dams can still be seen when the river is at its lowest stages.

Banks used a scorched-earth policy in his withdrawal, burning almost every building in the river towns as he retreated. Campti was utterly destroyed, and before he withdrew from Alexandria, Banks put it to the torch. No further Union expeditions plagued the now desolate valley, and the Trans-Mississippi area eventually became the last part of the Confederacy to surrender after Lee's disaster in the East.

Traffic on the river revived after the war and quickly surpassed its prewar level as more land was brought into cultivation. In 1880, there were eighteen boats in regular Red River service, making 165 trips to New Orleans. The Red River Line dominated traffic on the river after 1865 and struggled to meet the competition of the railroads after Shreveport was joined by them to Dallas in 1873, to New Orleans in 1882, and to Vicksburg in 1884. The struggle was a losing one. Within one year after the completion of the Texas and Pacific Railroad to New Orleans, it had won almost 60 percent of the total cotton transported from the valley, and the steamer traffic went into precipitous decline. In 1896, the Red River Line operated only six boats between Shreveport and New Orleans; yet as late as 1911 an old veteran of the line, the *W. T. Scovell*, still plied the river.

Most of the valley towns and cities continued to grow and prosper after the coming of the railroad, but some, such as Sibley's Landing and Port

Caddo, are gone. The names of Mooringsport and Shreveport bring back nostalgic memories of great days on the Red. Cities such as Alexandria and Shreveport, created because of the river, now thrive without it.

The river did not die without mourners, and there are many who await its revival. The Red River Valley Association, formed in 1925 with members in a four-state area, has worked diligently and with considerable success to persuade the national government to make the river useful to man again. Huge flood-control reservoirs have been built at Dennison and Texarkana in Texas, and at Bodcau and Wallace lakes in Louisiana. But paramount in the aims of the Association has been the restoration of water transportation for the valley. Though the river itself cannot be restored to commercial usefulness, in 1946 the Congress approved the idea of constructing a barge canal lateral to the Red River, the Overton–Red River Waterway. Surveys and feasibility studies bear out the wisdom of such a project. While funds for it have not yet been appropriated, the valley may someday hear the chug of a diesel tug shoving a tow of barges through channels abandoned by the Red centuries ago. When it does, the old Red River will come alive again in its new body.

Minden Chamber of Commerce

Bayou Dorcheat

Louisiana Tourist Development Commission

Lake Bistineau

Louisiana Department of Agriculture

Log Cabin, Old German Colony, Near Minden

Shreveport Chamber of Commerce

Shreveport

Shreveport Waterfront, Circa Early 1890's

Courtesy Mrs. Henry Jolly

Firemen's Parade, Shreveport, Circa 1880's

Natchitoches, 1864

Frank Leslie's Illustrated Newspaper

The Occupation of Alexandria, 1863

Harper's Magazine

Logjam on Red River, 1872

Removal of Logjam on Red River, 1872

Centenary College Library

Red River Below Shreveport, 1872

Centenary College Library

Red River Commerce

Louisiana Department of Agriculture

Louisiana Department of Commerce and Industry

Red River Above Alexandria

Part III | *Southwest Louisiana*

The Sabine

By RALEIGH A. SUAREZ

WHERE THE SABINE RIVER enters Louisiana at a point 32° N. latitude and 94° W. longitude, the middle of the river becomes the Louisiana-Texas boundary. After flowing on a southeasterly course for about 150 miles and then turning toward the southwest for another 150 miles or so, the river finally enters the Gulf of Mexico via Sabine Lake and Sabine Pass.

For the most part, the river flows swiftly around one sharp bend after another along a narrow, sinuous channel which often has a sandbar on one side and a caving bank on the other. Sometimes, however, there are long stretches of slow-moving water. Then the stream has gently sloping banks covered with overhanging trees. Here and there along its course, the river strikes the hills bordering its valley and forms bluffs that sometimes are over a hundred feet high. But the elevation of the riverbanks adjacent to the "first bottoms" decreases gradually from about thirty feet near Logansport to almost nothing at Sabine Lake.

The average width of the river from Logansport south for about 200 miles is 100 feet. As the river continues on its southern course, it widens to an average of 200 feet, with extreme widths of 400 feet in a few places. But at the Narrows, a 17-mile-long, crooked, narrow passage which begins about 20 miles north of Orange, the channel is restricted to half its width. Below the Narrows, the river averages 300 feet in width and attains a breadth of 500 feet at Orange and 1,000 feet near Sabine Lake. Probably the average width of the river in its entire Louisiana course is between 100 feet and 150 feet.

In a number of places between Logansport and Pearl Creek, ledges of rock or very hard clay pass partly across the river, confine it to half its normal width, and cause considerable acceleration of the river's current. When these ledges run entirely across the river, as they do in several places, rapids are formed. The most pronounced rapids are the Mc-

Clanahan Shoals at the mouth of Bayou Negreet and the Goodwin or Gordon Shoals near Columbus. The McClanahan Shoals, according to one observer, are "about a quarter of a mile long and in low water is quiet [*sic*] dangerous for even small boats." The Goodwin or Gordon Shoals, however, are probably the most extensive on the river. Other noteworthy shoals are those at Bayou Nana, Stone Coal Bluff, and Anthony Ferry.

Sabine Lake, into which the river flows, is almost oval in shape and covers approximately 100 square miles. Its long axis is 18 miles in a northeast-southwest direction to the head of Sabine Pass. The lake's short axis is 7½ miles in a northwest-southeast direction. Sabine Pass, the narrow, slightly sinuous outlet of Sabine Lake into the Gulf of Mexico, is almost 6⅓ air-line miles long and averages a half mile in width.

Although the Sabine River is said to have been "deep enough during the flood season to have been navigated by steamboats transporting freight in the late 1800's as far north as Logansport," widespread use of the stream as a major avenue of transportation was impractical. The numerous shoals hindered navigation in any except the high-water period. For example, when the river gauged a depth of 18 feet, the water above McClanahan Shoals measured but 6 inches. At times, log rafts also halted river traffic. In 1837, for instance, the shipment of supplies to Camp Sabine, about 14 miles from Many, was delayed because of a logjam located approximately 100 miles above Orange. Although this raft was cleared in 1838, it had reformed before 1840 and was over two miles long. In the 1860's, a raft in the same area halted all traffic. Obviously, low water, shoals, rapids, and log rafts did much to isolate the Sabine Valley.

The Sabine River is the western boundary of a portion of DeSoto Parish and is the western limit of Sabine, Vernon, Beauregard, Calcasieu, and Cameron parishes. Since the Sabine River failed to attract waves of settlers to its valley, western Louisiana was sparsely populated prior to the Civil War; and, as late as 1880, the Sabine River Valley was considered "too little known and settled to attract attention." Today, of the parishes adjacent to the Sabine River, only Calcasieu is thickly populated. The others rank among those parishes with the lowest density of population. Four of these six parishes (Cameron, Vernon, Sabine, and DeSoto) suffered population losses between 1940 and 1950. The population of Beauregard and Calcasieu parishes increased during the same period, but the river had nothing to do with their growth.

By 1950, only three cities in the area were peopled by over 5,000 persons. Two of the three were located in Calcasieu Parish, where an industrial complex had developed along the banks of the lower Calcasieu River. The third, DeRidder, in north-central Beauregard Parish, gained little from the Sabine or its valley.

Events of the 1950's brought insignificant changes. Beauregard and Calcasieu continued to grow; Cameron's population increased slightly. But DeSoto, Sabine, and Vernon continued to lose people. Lake Charles, Sulphur, and DeRidder were joined by Mansfield, in DeSoto Parish, in the class of cities with a population exceeding 5,000.

Before the Civil War, these parishes provided homes for yeomen and subsistence farmers, cattle grazers, and a few timbermen. Therefore, with the exception of DeSoto Parish, each was predominantly white, a characteristic which remains today.

Of the parishes, only Calcasieu can be considered urban; and two, Cameron and Sabine, must be ranked with the most rural in the State. However, only a minority of the labor force, even in the five rural parishes, depends upon agriculture for a livelihood. Furthermore, the urban portion of the population of each parish is increasing.

Investigation reveals that the Sabine River has played only a minor role in the economic progress made by the people of this area. Mineral production, primarily petroleum and natural gas, and timber and timber products have accounted for most of the economic growth of the rural parishes. The enormous industrial developments in Calcasieu Parish cannot be linked with the Sabine River.

Although the Sabine River has played a negligible role in the economic development of western Louisiana, it is a source of fresh water, an extremely valuable natural resource, which Louisianians long have taken for granted. For generations, the water resources of the State have been wasted and misused. By the middle of the twentieth century, however, Louisianians were aware of the "grave public need" for the conservation of the fresh waters of the State.

Therefore, the Sabine River's potential was recognized, and Louisianians and Texans together began studies to determine whether or not the construction of a dam on the Sabine River would alleviate some of the problems caused by the ever increasing freshwater shortage in western Louisiana and eastern Texas. This effort revealed that such a dam was "economically sound and feasible," and the two states developed plans for the construction of Toledo Bend Dam. The project was to cost $54,500,000, a sum which was adjudged reasonable when the potential benefits were considered.

Proponents of the dam maintain that it will: (1) provide priceless water for the industry already in South Louisiana; (2) attract paper mills and other new industries; (3) increase the minimum flow of the Sabine River, thereby improving its capacity to dispose of industrial waste; and (4) draw smaller industries because of the recreational opportunity and scenic beauty that will be developed. Authorities also believe that the dam will provide: (1) *Irrigation* for thousands of acres of Louisiana rice now jeopardized by salt-water intrusion; (2) *Employment* opportunities in an area where economic depression has resulted in population decreases; (3) *Recreation* for millions of Louisiana residents and tourists; (4) *Flood Control* for the Sabine River watershed; and (5) *Electric Power* for Louisiana industry. Members of the Louisiana Sabine River Authority claim that the "Navigation potential of the Sabine River [will be] greatly increased."

Obviously, if all these benefits are realized, life for western Louisiana residents will be changed tremendously. But even if some of these claims are unattainable, realization of the other benefits will lead to increased prosperity for the area.

What will result from Toledo Bend Dam remains to be seen. Therefore, no stretch of the imagination will permit consideration of the Sabine River as a great river. Its narrow Louisiana valley has provided sustenance for no important industrial or agricultural developments; its sinuous channel has been a highway for but few persistent seekers of greener pastures; its banks have proved slight barriers for the thousands of Americans who have moved farther westward in quest of fertile soil. Until now, as far as Louisiana is concerned, the Sabine River just runs its course, contributing but little to the wealth and well-being of the inhabitants of its environs.

Nevertheless, the Sabine has been important and has been the focal point of the thoughts and actions of many men. Obviously, size has had nothing to do with the importance of the river; and although sections of the river and its hinterland are beautiful, natural beauty has had little effect on the significance of the area. Thus the Sabine gained no fame from its length, breadth, or depth; no glory from its aesthetic qualities; and no accolades for its contributions to the material well-being of its people.

Importance grew from geography and history. At one time or another in the past 250 years, the Sabine has been on the frontier of empires, nations, and states. Through the years Spaniards, Frenchmen, Americans, Texans, and Louisianians have argued, threatened, and fought about the valley of the Sabine. The Sabine, therefore, was important because it was where it was, not because of what it was.

From the first quarter of the eighteenth century when the forces of France and Spain collided in western Louisiana until the first quarter of the nineteenth century when the boundary between Louisiana and Spanish Texas was settled, the Sabine frontier was an area whose fate was a part of the high stakes played for at the table of diplomatic chance. But the forces contending for the area knew little more about the Sabine River than its general location. Seemingly, that was all that the powers wanted to know. As early as 1715, for example, the royal French geographer was told to make no indication of the westernmost extent of Louisiana because even

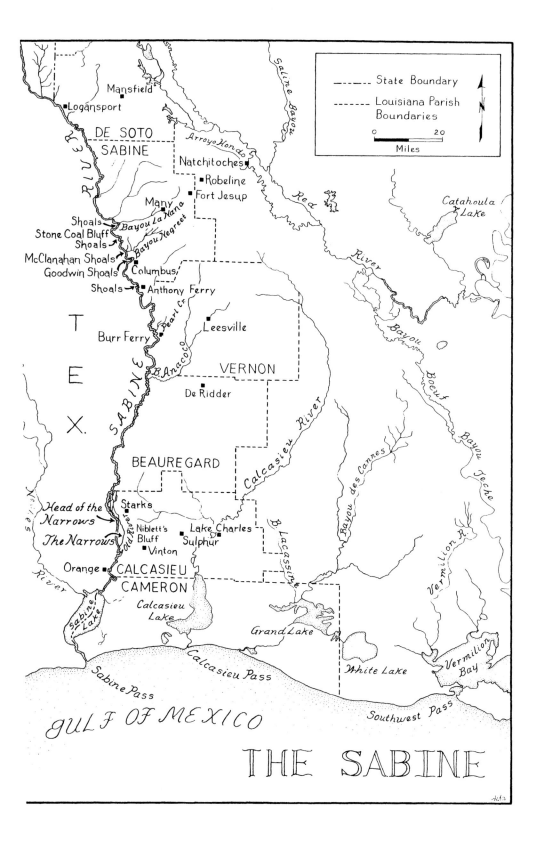

such a tentative delineation would allow "foreign nations [to] use our maps against us when we discuss important questions with them."

Nevertheless, much was learned about western Louisiana and eastern Texas between 1715 and 1821, but accurate information about the Sabine River was not included in the body of facts available to geographers, politicians, and historians. The first correct idea of the general shape and location of the Sabine was not available until 1816, when William Darby's map of Louisiana was published. There, the river was represented "by the conventional wavy line." Not until 1837 was a map to show the shape of the bends of the river with any accuracy. Public land surveys completed between 1830 and 1879, however, did result in river and area maps of varying degrees of accuracy. Nevertheless, it was not until 1902 that a truly accurate map of the Sabine River became available. Thus, as far as the Sabine was concerned, knowledge that the river was there appears to have been sufficient.

The attitude toward the land immediately east of the Sabine Valley was entirely different. French and Spanish contention for the area resulted in the establishment of forts and missions; and for a time, the Presidio del Nuestra Señora del Pilar de Los Adaes, near modern Robeline, was the capital of the royal province of Texas. Nearby French Natchitoches, of course, was the oldest permanent settlement in what is now Louisiana.

French-Spanish conflict over control of western Louisiana diminished after 1721; but from time to time until 1753, when the Spanish appear to have accepted the Arroyo Hondo as the eastern limit of Texas—a solution which seems to have been acceptable to the French—the border question arose. From 1753 to 1803, the western extent of Louisiana was not under question. But when Napoleon Bonaparte sold Louisiana to the United States, the boundary problem returned with increased complexity. The United States did not know what she had bought; if France knew what she had sold, she would not tell. The third party involved, Spain, felt that she had been a victim of a French coup and was determined to maintain her position in what she considered to be eastern Texas.

Thus, Spain placed the boundary between Louisiana and Texas no farther west than a line southward along the Arroyo Hondo and the Calcasieu River. The United States disagreed and claimed that the western limit of Louisiana reached at least to the Sabine River and possibly to the Rio Grande. These points of view had to be reconciled, if conflict were to be prevented. The spirit of compromise prevailed. In 1806, a Neutral Ground was created between the Sabine River on the west and the Arroyo Hondo and the line of the Calcasieu River on the east.

In the decade and a half of its existence, the Neutral Ground was the refuge of desperados as well as the home of honest, although trespassing, squatters who tried to clear land for cultivation. As time passed and the outlaws in the strip became bolder, they plundered and robbed travelers along El Camino Real, the highway west from Natchitoches to Mexico.

Therefore, in 1810, a joint Spanish-American force moved into the Neutral Ground and temporarily curbed the depredations of the outlaws. Unfortunately, since it was impossible to distinguish the honest from the unlawful, many peaceful squatters saw their homes destroyed by destructive fires set by the invading force. Since the success of the expedition was short-lived, the criminal element soon renewed its plundering and killing. Not until after 1821 did the area cease to be the haven of the outlaw. Yet, even with the extension of American law to the area, outlawry continued for years.

The Adams-Onis Treaty, which was ratified in 1821, established the west bank of the Sabine River as a part of the boundary between Spanish Texas and Louisiana. The west bank remained a part of the western boundary of the United States and of Louisiana until after Texas was annexed to the Union. In 1848, the boundary between Texas and Louisiana was moved from the west bank to the center of the river.

As indicated earlier, controversies over ownership of western Louisiana led to the establishment of military outposts. At intervals after 1821, some of these strongholds gained prominence. When Texas fought for and gained her independence, for example, Fort Jesup, eight miles west of Robeline, and Camp Sabine, fourteen miles from Many, became significant military posts. Fort Jesup's greatest hour, however, came during the Mexican War when it became the jumping-off point for many of the American troops moving through Texas to Mexico.

From the close of the Mexican War until the opening of the Civil War, military interest in the Sabine area waned; but, with the coming of that great struggle, the stream again began to figure in the military plans of army commanders. After the fall of New Orleans, Union forces began attempts to gain control of Texas. The North's "most desperate effort," according to some Texans, "was made at Sabine Pass in September 1863." The Federal force of gunboats and transports got as far as Sabine Pass, where a small Confederate force of forty-seven men under Lieutenant Richard W. Dowling forced the withdrawal of the large Federal force. As one Texan put it, "Without the loss of a man, the little band of soldiers had killed more than one hundred Federal soldiers and had captured two gunboats and three hundred and fifty men."

Thus, history and geography have made the area important. But the future importance of the Sabine country must rest upon what Louisianians and Texans do to develop its potential. A project like Toledo Bend Dam should be a beginning, not an ending. Texans have built industrial complexes on the lower Sabine River; Louisianians have done nothing of consequence. If the Sabine River is to contribute to the economic well-being of Louisianians, some of the projected benefits of Toledo Bend Dam must be realized. Furthermore, Louisianians in the Sabine Valley must take greater advantage of the area's natural beauty and historic past. If this is done, western Louisiana might one day become an important recreational center. If the people in the Sabine Valley of Louisiana are able to take advantage of the resources of their area, the valley should become far more prosperous, productive, and attractive.

The Calcasieu

By A. OTIS HEBERT, JR.

THE FIRST MAIN RIVER wholly within Louisiana after one enters the State from the west is the Calcasieu. The word "Calcasieu" is an Indian name meaning "crying eagle." The Calcasieu River originates in Vernon Parish and from there begins on a southeasterly flow into Rapides Parish, then turns gradually to a southwesterly flow through the parishes of Allen, Jefferson Davis, Calcasieu, and Cameron. In Cameron the river enters Calcasieu Lake, a body of fresh water fifteen miles long and approximately four miles wide. The principal tributaries of the Calcasieu River are Devils Creek, Bundicks Creek, Beckwith Creek, Whiskey Chitto Creek, Six Mile Creek, Ten Mile Creek, Bayou Choupique, and Houston River. On some of the early maps of the region the Calcasieu was noted by other names, the most common being "Bayou Quelqueshue" and "Culeashue."

Like most of the streams in the area, the Calcasieu River, in the early days of the history of Louisiana was obstructed with snags, logs, fallen trees, and sandbars. This situation was especially true above the present city of Lake Charles, beginning near present-day Jones Bluff, twenty-eight miles north of the city. South of Lake Charles the Calcasieu had an average depth of about 10 feet at low water and widths varying from 200 feet to 600 feet. At the entrance of Lake Calcasieu the river depth averaged only about 3 feet, and at the Calcasieu Pass the depth was between 5 feet and 6½ feet.

Thus, prior to the Civil War, commerce on the Calcasieu River was negligible. The war brought havoc to the area, just as it did to other parts of the State and to the South. Confederate money had become valueless, and business degenerated into barter. "Landings" developed along the Calcasieu River, where such products as cloth, coffee, salt, sugar, cornmeal were exchanged for lumber, livestock, and hides. One trading vessel, the sloop *Emma,* took lumber and cowhides to Galveston and brought back salt, bacon, flour, pepper, furniture, and chinaware, as well as pants, shirts, shotguns, powder, and shot. These landings in some cases later grew into villages and towns.

In the years immediately following the Civil War, two events occurred to make the river one of the most important rivers in southwest Louisiana— the opening of the lumbering industry on a large commercial basis and the extension of the Southern Pacific Railroad into the area, which stimulated migration of people into the region. At first many were apprehensive of the railroad, fearing it would damage water commerce, but these skeptics were soon convinced that their fears were for naught. Not only did the railroad stimulate the population of the region, it also stimulated water commerce by facilitating transportation of produce to the river for foreign export.

The first important item of trade was lumber. Schooners plying the waters of the Calcasieu took cargoes of lumber to Galveston, which for a long time was the most important trading center for Calcasieu River products. In exchange for this lumber, the ships brought back supplies and food products. Even though Galveston was the main trading center for ships of the Calcasieu River, a large portion of the products imported from Galveston had originally come from New Orleans, since regular steamship service between the two cities had been established as early as the 1850's.

In 1869, Captain John Miller attempted to establish direct connection with New Orleans, but this venture seems to have been unsuccessful, since ten years later a Lake Charles newspaper reported that Galveston was still the principal trading point of Calcasieu commerce.

As the area became more populated and as commerce increased, efforts were made to clear obstructions from the river. In 1872, the channel at the head of Calcasieu Pass was deepened to 5 feet wide and 8 feet deep. But a year later this channel was useless. In 1881, another channel 70 feet wide and 8 feet deep was dredged. This was later made 100 feet wide and 6 feet deep, and was protected by a plank revetment on each side. A channel of similar dimensions was also dredged at the head of Calcasieu Lake. Again, in 1892, an 80-foot channel was dredged and jetties built, but all these had little effect. It was not until 1926 that the present deepwater channel, 100 feet wide and 40 feet deep, was built connecting Lake Charles to the Gulf of Mexico thirty-five miles away. Presently this channel is again being widened and deepened.

Trade with foreign countries was difficult because Lake Charles was not a port of entry. Thus duties had to be paid elsewhere, in this case Brashear City, which was the port of entry for a number of Gulf ports. Foreign capitalists, particularly the French, were interested in purchasing lumber supplies from the Calcasieu country but were hamstrung by this handicap. In 1880, the United States Congress, upon petition from area citizens, authorized the Secretary of the Treasury to appoint a deputy collector at Lake Charles; but none was named. In 1889, area citizens again petitioned, and the following year a deputy collector was appointed and located at Calcasieu Pass.

During the early days of the settlement of the Gulf Coast area, the present region of southwest Louisiana remained undisturbed. Certainly the land was sighted by some of the early Gulf explorers and possibly visited. Roger Baudier, in his monumental history of *The Catholic Church in Louisiana,* tells a story, undoubtedly legend, of an early Dominican missionary, Brother Marcos de Mena, who along with three hundred others was shipwrecked on the Gulf Coast. According to the tale, the survivors were attacked by Indians, and Brother de Mena was wounded by several arrows. His companions, not daring to tarry longer than necessary and fearing another Indian attack, buried Brother de Mena in a shallow grave. Since he was not quite dead at the time, an opening was left so that the good Brother could breathe. The story goes that Brother de Mena did not die, but somehow managed to regain his strength and work his way out of his premature entombment. After finding his companions all slain by Indians, he eventually made his way to the City of Mexico.

In the early days of European America the area of southwest Louisiana was referred to as "Attakapas Country," after the wandering tribes of Indians that roamed its rivers and bayous. It was in 1818 that the first map appeared listing the area as "Calcasieu Country," the name given to it by the Spanish conquistadores in the middle of the 1700's. Throughout the entire colonial period, during both French and Spanish dominations, the region remained primarily Indian country. The main Indian group occupying southwest Louisiana was the Attakapa. It is believed that they possessed the lowest cultural level of any of the Indian tribes inhabiting present-day Louisiana. One tribe, the Assinais, is believed to have been the only cannibalistic tribe to roam over Louisiana. Even though the Calcasieu country was the last area of Louisiana to be densely populated by whites, the only Indian contributions are a few names given to rivers, bayous, and geographic locations, such as "Calcasieu" and "Mermentau." Today the Koasati Indians, members of the Coushatta Tribe who live in Allen Parish, are the only Indians left in the area. And strangely, they were not originally from any region of the State; rather, they migrated into Louisiana from Alabama over a century and a half ago.

When the United States purchased Louisiana from France in 1803, the indefinite boundaries caused difficulties with Spain, which at the time was in possession of Texas. Spain claimed the western boundary of Louisiana was the Arroyo Hondo and Calcasieu rivers; the United States claimed an exaggerated boundary to the Rio Grande. For years the area between the Sabine on the west and Arroyo Hondo and Calcasieu on the east remained a "No Man's Land" occupied by adventurers, murderers, desperadoes, hijackers, cutthroats, and robbers. The disputed area also held an appeal for Jean Laffite and his band of privateers who roamed the Gulf shores from their base, originally at Barataria and later at Galveston. It is said that Laffite buried some of his treasures along the banks of the Calcasieu, and even in recent times people have searched for them. The area also served as a convenient point of entry for the smuggling of slaves by Laffite after the foreign slave trade was outlawed in 1808.

A fort in No Man's Land was established at Niblett's Bluff, near the present town of Vinton. Here cattle drivers rested their herds of Texas Longhorns on the way to New Orleans and other marketplaces in the East. Another fort was built on the banks of Charles Lake and named "Cantonment Atkinson" in honor of Brigadier General Henry Atkinson, who was in command of the western division of the United States Army. The fort was located at what is now the foot of Lawrence Street in the city of Lake Charles. It overlooked the lake and river and commanded the passage to the woods in the rear. In 1832, Cantonment Atkinson was abandoned, and at the turn of the century the fifteen-room building was torn down. All that remains today to note the spot is a granite marker donated by the Daughters of the American Revolution. The land on which the fort stood was sold to James Barnett, who in turn sold it to Thomas Bilbo, a French-Canadian who became the first surveyor of Calcasieu Parish. Tradition has it that both Antonio López de Santa Anna and Sam Houston, the two antagonists at the Battle of San Jacinto, were entertained at Cantonment Atkinson.

The Calcasieu was inhabited by white people before the American Revolution. They were attracted not only by the beauty of the land but by the open prairies which provided excellent pasture for livestock. Martin LeBleu, who settled on the banks of English Bayou about 1770, is believed to be the first settler attracted to the area. LeBleu came from Virginia but was originally from Bordeaux, France. It is said that LeBleu and his wife made the journey in a two-wheel cart and that when she came to the land of the Calcasieu, Mrs. LeBleu became so enamored of the moss-draped oaks and the drooping cypresses that she persuaded her husband to settle there.

On the west side of the Calcasieu, also before the American Revolution, Louis Reon built himself a house on Bayou D'Inde. Other settlers in the region at this time included Henry Moss, Jacob Ryan, and Pierre Vincent. All of these settlers received Spanish land grants, and because of the uncertainty of the boundary after the acquisition of the land by the United States, these settlers continued to pay land taxes to the Spanish governor at Nacogdoches, Texas, until 1819, when the Adams-Onis Treaty definitely

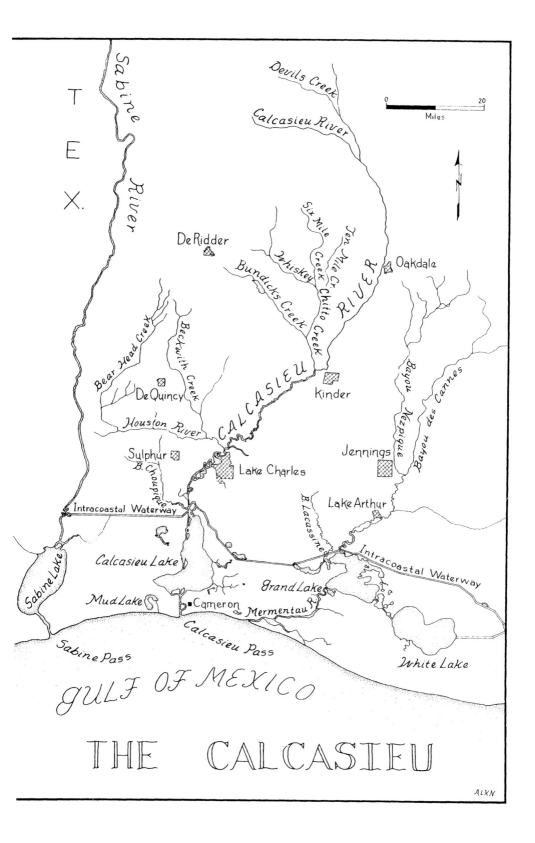

established United States sovereignty over the area. The Vincent home still stands today, but the homes of the other early settlers have been replaced by the massive steel structures of Firestone, Cities Service, and other plants that make the great industrial complex which has sprung up along the banks of the Calcasieu River, Calcasieu Lake, and Charles Lake.

About 1800, Charles Sallier, with a Spanish land grant, built the first home within what is the present city of Lake Charles. In the early days it was customary to call a man by his Christian name; hence, Charles Sallier was referred to as "Monsieur Charles." So the lake which was overlooked by his land and home came to be called "Charles Lake." His name is also preserved in Sallier Street in Lake Charles.

During the border dispute with Spain over the Calcasieu country, in order to hold off the Spaniards, the United States Government offered homesteads to anyone willing to move to, and settle in, the region. This enticement brought a new group of settlers—homesteaders from the other southern states. Heretofore, most of the settlers had been French and Spanish and a few Acadians. Among the newcomers were John Henderson, Dempsey Iles, David Choate, and Joshua Johnson. Settlement of the dispute over the "Neutral Strip" increased migration into the area, bringing, among others, John Bryan, father of J. W. Bryan, the first mayor of Lake Charles; Richard West; William Praither; James Hodges; and Alexander Hebert. For years these people had to travel to Opelousas to attend court and to vote, since they were part of "Imperial St. Landry." This trip required two weeks on horseback. These inhabitants, understandably, yearned for a parish of their own.

Their desire was fulfilled in 1840 when Calcasieu Parish was carved out of St. Landry. Now larger than the mother parish, Calcasieu was dubbed "Imperial Calcasieu." But she, too, lost her imperial status in 1912 when the parishes of Allen, Beauregard, and Jefferson Davis were carved from her area. Imperial Calcasieu contained six thousand square miles and had over two thousand inhabitants.

The first parish seat was Marion, six miles from present-day Lake Charles. This site was selected principally because it was on the Old Spanish Trail from New Orleans to Texas. In 1852, largely at the insistence of Jacob Ryan, Jr., the parish seat was moved to Lake Charles. Ryan had seen the possibilities of the settlement on the east bank, moved there, and agitated for the parish seat. In 1852, the State Legislature gave its approval, saying it did not care where the seat of justice was located so long as it did not involve any expense to the State. The courthouse and jail were placed on ox-drawn wagons, transported to Lake Charles, and placed on the same square where the present courthouse stands. The location site was donated by Jacob Ryan; his trading-post partner, James Hodges; and the city's first lawyer, Samuel Adams Kirby. It is no wonder that Jacob Ryan is known as "The Father of Lake Charles."

Uncle Jake, as he was known to his contemporaries, operated a sawmill on the lakefront. He also sold most of the property on what is today Ryan Street by the rope length. Thus, lumbering was the first industry of the region. The industry received a stimulus in the middle 1850's when Captain Daniel Goos moved to Lake Charles and applied improved methods of lumbering. Goos also owned the first steamboat to regularly operate out of Lake Charles.

The lumbering industry was interrupted by the Civil War, just as was every other activity. However, by the end of Reconstruction in 1877, there were a dozen sawmills in the region. Trade and communication still were primarily by water, and Texas cities continued to be the principal outlet. Life was very simple in the still-pioneer region. Overland travel was by horseback, wagon, or buggy. Generally, only male members of the family traveled, and then usually in groups for protection. Even though the border dispute with Spain had long been settled, there remained bandits who plagued the Old Spanish Trail to Opelousas, Vermilionville (Lafayette), and St. Martinville. Roads were of dirt, and each ward had its own overseer appointed by the police jury.

Regional characteristics did not develop in the Calcasieu area until the 1880's. In this decade the lumbering activities which had developed modestly before the Civil War boomed. Also about that time came the first influx of Midwesterners, which gave the Calcasieu a characteristic distinct from the rest of southern Louisiana. These people brought with them the rice culture for which the region is still famous today. There were, however, other developments which contributed to the economic development of southwest Louisiana after 1880. Midwesterners also improved the cattle industry by introducing scientific breeding. Building of the Southern Pacific Railroad, as previously mentioned, did much to make the region accessible. Introduction of banks, both State and Federal, helped to alleviate the paucity of money.

That southwest Louisiana should witness a boom was as inevitable as modern Louisiana's undergoing industrialization. Over a half-century ago, William Henry Perrin in *Southwest Louisiana, Biographical and Historical,* stated: "Southwest Louisiana is a beautiful country. No man ought to desire a more lovely or richer country. It possesses everything necessary to wealth and the enjoyment of life. No extremes of climate are known here. No burning suns, no frozen snows, no chilling winds are felt. A healthful atmosphere, purified by the gulf breeze, prevails throughout the year. What then does it lack? Nothing but enterprise to properly develop it, and to let the outside world know what is here."

To three men primarily belongs the credit for the boom which took place in southwest Louisiana in the period after political Reconstruction—Jabez B. Watkins, Seaman A. Knapp, and Sylvester L. Cary. Watkins, entrepreneur land speculator, came to the Calcasieu country from Lawrence, Kansas, in 1883. Backed by English capital, he purchased much of the prairie and marshland available between the Sabine and Vermilion rivers. He purchased the land for its timber, but the company reclaimed as much of the marshland as it could and converted it into rice land. In this endeavor Watkins was greatly aided by his brother-in-law, Alexander Thomson, who left a professorship of mechanical engineering at Iowa State College, and by Seaman A. Knapp, former president of Iowa State College. Dr. Knapp, who formerly lived in Vinton, Iowa, was a pioneer in the development of the rice industry. He founded the "Boys Corn Club," which was a forerunner of the 4-H Clubs of America. Dr. Knapp also laid out the towns of Vinton and Iowa. He founded the Calcasieu Bank, which is today the Calcasieu-Marine Bank. It was Joseph Fabacher, a German, who is credited with cultivating the "first large field of rice ever grown in Southwest Louisiana," as well as introducing the first rice-threshing machine.

Watkins was instrumental in building the first north-south railroad in the section. The Watkins Railroad later became a part of the Missouri-Pacific system. He also built the first bank in Lake Charles, the Watkins Bank, which was financed largely by local people and was used in promoting immigration. Watkins was a nineteenth-century John Law in his promotional schemes. He founded the *American* newspaper and distributed copies throughout the United States and Europe to advertise his "Garden of Eden." He even purchased one thousand dollars' worth of one-cent stamps at one time to mail promotional literature in an effort to attract settlers to the Calcasieu country.

The third man in the triumvirate, Sylvester L. Cary, was a land agent of the Southern Pacific Railroad. After settling in Jennings, he became so captivated by the region that he launched a campaign to induce his fellow Midwesterners to seek their fortunes in the prairies of southwest Louisiana. Cary pointed out, by word of mouth and by the written word, the advantages of rice over wheat, primarily from the financial side. He showed that rice could yield twenty dollars per acre, whereas wheat would yield only five dollars per acre.

Another economic boost to the area was provided when sulphur was discovered near the city which bears its name. Sulphur began to be produced for commercial purposes in 1894. The town of Sulphur had been laid out in 1878 by Thomas Kleinpeter, a civil engineer. The first settlers were Acadians, but later families migrated from other southern states. The investors in the sulphur mine were New Yorkers, and it has been said that no other investment ever brought such great returns as did the Union Sulphur Company, with the possible exception of Ford Motor Company. In the 1920's, the supply of sulphur was exhausted, but now the company is developing one of the largest oil fields in the South.

From the present-day point of view, the outstanding achievement of the area was the deepwater channel which has been dug to connect Lake Charles with the Gulf of Mexico. Lake Charles has now become the third largest port in Louisiana. From this port leave rice, salt, cotton, lumber, and paper for all parts of the world. It is important to note that the port of Lake Charles ships more rice than any other port in America. And, with the deepwater channel, came the many industries which have made the Calcasieu River and Calcasieu Lake area the great industrial complex that it is today. The Mathieson alkali works, located here in 1933; and later came Continental Oil Refinery, Swift and Company, Cities Service refinery, Firestone Tire and Rubber Company, and many others.

Another Lake Charles industry remains to be mentioned. Its product is not chemical, rubber, lumber, or rice, but enlightened minds. This is McNeese State College, named after John McNeese, an early teacher in the area who as superintendent of schools left an indelible imprint on the development of education in the region.

Orange Chamber of Commerce

Lower Sabine River at Orange, Texas

Section of Chesapeake Bay Tunnel Under Tow, Lower Sabine River

Orange Chamber of Commerce

Offshore Rig No. 56 Under Tow, Lower Sabine River

Orange Chamber of Commerce

Camping at Sam Houston State Park

Louisiana Tourist Development Commission

Rice Mill, Lake Charles

Louisiana Department of Commerce and Industry

Louisiana Department of Commerce and Industry

Loading a Barge at Lake Charles

Tanker on the Calcasieu Ship Channel

Lake Charles Association of Commerce

Louisiana Department of Commerce and Industry

Tour of the Lake Charles Port

Part IV | *South Louisiana*

Bayou Teche

By ROBERT M. CRISLER

BAYOU TECHE is 123.9 miles in length from where it leaves Bayou Courtableau, at Port Barre, to where it joins the Atchafalaya River near Morgan City. General Richard Taylor, in his book *Destruction and Reconstruction,* published in 1879, called it the "loveliest of southern streams." It flows through the very heart of French Louisiana, better known as the "Cajun country."

"Teche" means "snake." Its meandering pattern closely resembles that of the Mississippi River. The Teche, in fact, about 3,000 years ago carried the amount of water the Mississippi carries today. The old course is still traceable northward through Bayou Courtableau, Bayou Wauksha, across Avoyelles Parish to Larto Lake in Catahoula Parish, and north of there to what is today the Tensas River.

The Red River flowed into the Teche, using the same route followed by Bayou Boeuf today—joining Bayou Cocodrie to form Bayou Courtableau north of present-day Washington, Louisiana, thence by way of Bayous Courtableau, Carron, and Mariecroquant into the present-day Teche between Leonville and Port Barre.

Today, most of the water carried by Bayou Boeuf and Bayou Cocodrie into Bayou Courtableau does not flow into the Teche at Port Barre, but enters the West Atchafalaya Basin Protection Levee borrow pit east of Port Barre. Some of this water rejoins the Teche at Charenton and is then diverted to the Gulf of Mexico at Baldwin by the Charenton Drainage and Navigation Canal.

Bayou Teche gently winds its way down the center of an alluvial ridge. The land slopes away from the natural levees on either side of the Teche, the land a few miles away on either side being five feet to ten feet lower in elevation. With the coming of the European, a "riverbank pattern" of settlement developed on the Teche, Courtableau, and Boeuf similar to that along the St. Lawrence River in Canada. Many long, narrow landholdings developed, with each settler building his home on the highest and best part right next to the bayou.

The lower Teche, from Breaux Bridge southeastward, is sugarcane country. Planting takes place in September, when stalks of cane are laid in the furrows and then covered. Shoots sprout from the joints of the stalks. The cane is harvested, almost entirely by machinery today, some fourteen months later in October. A second crop, from the same planting, is harvested a year later, and a third crop a year after that. Soybeans, to be plowed under to enrich the soil, are planted after the third crop is harvested. During the fall, large trucks carrying cane to the many mills that dot the landscape make rapid travel on the area highways an impossibility.

Most of the sugar mills merely produce raw brown sugar which is shipped out of the area for refining. The manufacturing of raw sugar is a relatively simple mechanical process. The cane is washed, then crushed, and the resulting juice is moved through a series of evaporating tanks. A stalk of sugarcane ends up as about a tablespoonful of sugar. By-products include blackstrap molasses, sold mostly for cattle feed, and leftover cane residue, known as bagasse, which can be made into many products, including wallboard and paper.

The upper Teche—from Breaux Bridge northward, and including the Boeuf-Cocodrie-Courtableau area—is cotton, corn, and cattle country. However, hot peppers, okra, cabbages, and sweet potatoes are of some local importance. One of the most unusual products of the Bayou Teche country is the crawfish. Breaux Bridge, with a 1960 population of 3,303, claims to be the "Crawfish Capital of the World." Ordinarily caught in the swamps and marshes, crawfish are now being raised commercially in flooded fields to meet the demands of an expanding market.

At the 1966 annual Crawfish Festival in Breaux Bridge, Andrew Thevenet ate $31\frac{1}{2}$ pounds of crawfish to retain his title of Champion Crawfish Eater, although he had eaten 33 pounds a year earlier. At this same festival, a crawfish called "Tee Louis," owned by Ray Broussard, won the crawfish races.

The Cajuns, or Acadians, who inhabit the lands adjacent to Bayou Teche are descendants of French settlers deported in 1755 from that section of Canada then known as Acadia, now Nova Scotia. They settled between 1765 and 1780 around the two trading posts that existed in the area, Poste Des Attakapas (now St. Martinville) and Poste Des Opelousas (now Opelousas).

This migration became the basis for the famous poem *Evangeline*, published in 1849 by Henry Wadsworth Longfellow, in which two young lovers, Evangeline and Gabriel, are deported from Acadia in separate ships. In the poem, Evangeline searches for Gabriel and finally finds him dying in her arms in a charity hospital in Philadelphia. Earlier in the poem, when Evangeline reached the home of Gabriel's father just after her lover had departed, she wept bitterly under a large oak tree on Bayou Teche. This tree, known as the "Evangeline Oak," is today a popular tourist attraction in St. Martinville.

The more popular version of the Evangeline story in the "Cajun country" is that the two young lovers were Emmeline Labiche and Louis Arceneaux. Arceneaux came to Bayou Teche first and married another woman. Emmeline, arriving three years later, met Louis under the Evangeline Oak, found he was already married, and died shortly thereafter of a broken heart.

Evangeline, or Emmeline Labiche, may be the heroine of the Teche country, but Jim Bowie of Opelousas is the legendary hero. Separating fact from fiction is not easy regarding this frontiersman, but he apparently cut a wide swath across Louisiana and Texas as a champion alligator rider, merchant, politician, planter, cattleman, slave smuggler, and duelist. He is also famed as a champion gambler, land speculator, Indian fighter, hero of the Alamo, and as inventor of the Bowie knife.

James Bowie was born in Logan County, Kentucky, in 1796. His family moved from there to Missouri and later, in 1802, to Louisiana. Between 1814 and 1819, he was apparently engaged in clearing land on Bayou Boeuf, sawing lumber and barging it to New Orleans. He sold his land in 1819, and went into the slave-smuggling business, his source of slaves being another legendary hero, Jean Laffite. After this, and until he moved to Texas in 1828, it is probably safe to say he was primarily a land speculator, although among other activities he was associated with his brother, Rezin Bowie, Jr., in developing "Arcadia," a sugar plantation just south of Thibodaux. Rezin married Margarite Neville in Opelousas, in 1814, and lived just south of Opelousas during the period 1815-1824.

James Bowie became a legend in 1827. A duel fought on a sandbar across the river from Natchez, Mississippi, turned into something of a free-for-all, with Bowie and his knife emerging famous, although the number killed and wounded in the melee has been generally and wildly exaggerated. Alexandria, rather than Opelousas, tended to be his business headquarters. Mississippi and Arkansas, as well as Louisiana, claim to be the site of the invention of the Bowie knife. Although he died, of course, with Davy Crockett and the others at the Alamo, Opelousas claims to be his hometown and promotes its Jim Bowie Museum and Tourist Center, next to the Jim Bowie Oak, on the main east-west street in the center of the city.

To get to Jim Bowie's part of the Teche country in the early period, one went up the Mississippi from New Orleans to where Plaquemine is today, thence by way of Bayou Plaquemine to the Atchafalaya, then into Bayou Courtableau and up the Courtableau to Washington. Evangeline's part of the

Teche country could be reached in the same manner, except that one followed the Atchafalaya down to the mouth of the Teche and up Bayou Teche to St. Martinville. During periods of low water the journey had to be made all the way up the Mississippi to its junction with the Red River, and then down the Atchafalaya from the Red River to the Courtableau or Teche.

Steamboats coming up the Teche to St. Martinville, in 1826, greatly reduced the problem of isolation. Further improvement in the accessibility of the area came with the completion of the railroad from New Orleans to Morgan City in 1857. But not until 1878 was the railroad extended to Lafayette. Branch lines were completed to St. Martinville and Opelousas in 1882.

Since the advent of the railroad and the paved highway, use of Bayou Teche for transportation has steadily declined. Navigation is still possible from Morgan City to Arnaudville, and there is some traffic, primarily clam shells and petroleum. St. Martinville has been far surpassed in size by Lafayette and New Iberia. Washington, former "boomtown" on the Courtableau, is now only the fifth largest city in St. Landry Parish.

The Indians who inhabited the Bayou Teche area, and southwest Louisiana generally, were primarily the Attakapa (sometimes called "Tuckapaw"). The Opelousas were closely related to them. On the lower Teche the native Indians were the Chitimachas. Choctaw and Alabamu Indians migrated into the Opelousas area after white settlement had begun. Through history, the Attakapa have been referred to as cannibals, but it is doubtful that they deserved this reputation; they neither attracted nor repelled white settlement. They fought with the army raised in 1779 by Bernardo de Gálvez, Spanish governor of Louisiana, for his expedition against the British-held fort at Baton Rouge. Some Indians registered cattle brands at the Poste Des Attakapas. In all of southwest Louisiana in 1698, there were only an estimated 1,750 Attakapa and related Indians; and, by 1805, this number had dropped to 175. No Attakapa remain today.

The only Indian reservation in Louisiana today is located on the lower Teche on the western edge of Charenton. The Indians here are descendants of the Chitimachas. The small area hardly rates continuance as a reservation, for the inhabitants have been almost completely assimilated by the Cajuns. They know few, if any, Chitimacha words, and they hardly look like Indians at all. To them, marriage with Negroes means being thrown out of the tribe. Unless one knows exactly where the reservation is located, it is easy to miss. A few years ago the writer asked one of the residents if he had anything in the house that might be uniquely "Indian." He said a woman came in, back in WPA days during the 1930's, to teach the reservation women to weave baskets. However, after searching his house, he was unable to find one of these baskets to show me.

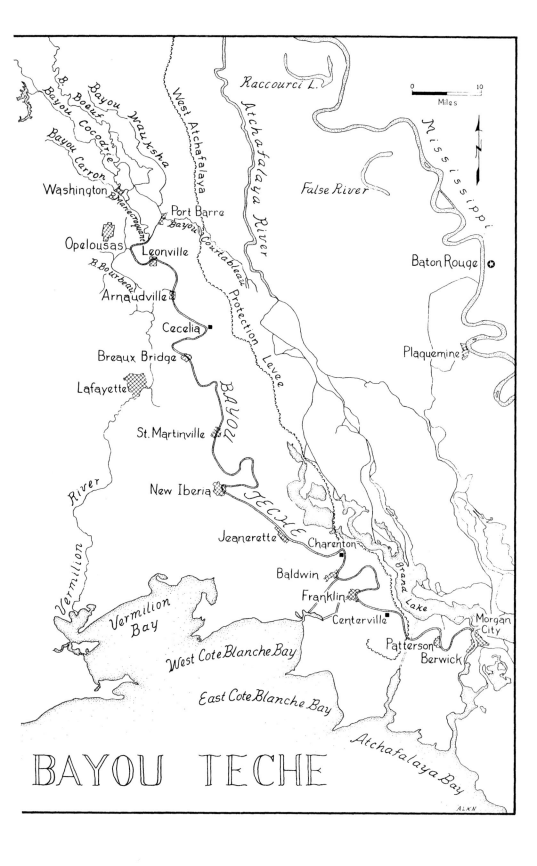

During the Civil War the Teche country was invaded by Federal troops, under General Nathaniel P. Banks, in the spring of 1863. The Confederate forces holding the Teche area were under General Richard Taylor. Badly outnumbered by the Federal forces advancing up the Teche, all Taylor could do was fight delaying actions and destroy all bridges as he retreated.

Banks assembled his forces in April at Brashear City (now Morgan City). Taylor was across the Atchafalaya entrenched on the Teche near its mouth. Banks planned a frontal attack with 10,000 men, and another 5,000 were sent by gunboats to Grand Lake to march to Franklin and cut off the retreat of the Confederates. Taylor, with some 4,000 men, learned of the flanking movement in time. After a day of heavy fighting, April 13, 1863, between Pattersonville (now Patterson) and Centreville (Battle of Bisland), he pulled back and engaged the flanking Federal force the next day at Irish Bend on the Teche (Battle of Franklin). The Federals lost about 225 men, killed or wounded, at Bisland and 350 more at Irish Bend; the Confederates had at least 150 killed, wounded, and captured. Banks, reaching Opelousas on April 20 and Alexandria on May 7, then marched east to lay seige to Port Hudson, which finally fell on July 9. He left behind a trail of general havoc in the Teche country.

Taylor and the Confederates, meanwhile, drove Federal forces back to the Mississippi River in northeast Louisiana and then moved back into the Teche country, capturing Brashear City on June 22. A month later Brashear City was again in the hands of the Federals, with the Confederates again retreating up the Teche.

In October, Federal General William B. Franklin advanced up the Teche with almost 20,000 men. Skirmishing began around Vermilionville (now Lafayette) on October 9, 1863. Thereafter, under constant harassment by the Confederates, the Federal forces reached Opelousas on October 21. However, the main Federal force withdrew to Vermilionville.

Confederates under Brigadier General Thomas Green attacked Federal forces left encamped south of Opelousas on November 4, 1863 (Battle of Bayou Bourbeau). While the Confederates suffered some 180 casualties, Federal losses included 25 killed, 129 wounded, and 562 captured or missing. At the end of 1863, the Federal forces were back in Brashear City, while Taylor was in Opelousas. The major action shifted the following year to the Red River Valley.

Confederate forces in the two Teche campaigns had some excellent leaders, such as Brigadier General Alfred Mouton and Brigadier General Thomas Green; leadership on the Federal side was generally less than inspired. However, desertions plagued the Confederates, while straggling and looting plagued the Federals. The destruction of property was staggering.

Today, the Teche country is rather densely populated. Not only have the few Indians been assimilated, but French and Spanish settlers were easily absorbed. For that matter, the "Americans" who have moved into the area have also been absorbed. The Cajuns are Roman Catholics, and until very recently the dominant language was French. They believe in large families, drink their coffee strong and often, love dancing and horseracing, and have a strong tendency to "stay put."

The author, speaking at a public school assembly in Arnaudville just a few years ago, was told by the principal of the school that the entire student body—first grade through twelfth—was Catholic. The only other Protestant in the gymnasium that day was the vocational agriculture teacher. Yet the dominant names in the Arnaudville telephone book sound less French than in most places in the Teche country.

Most numerous family names in some of the current telephone books are as follows:

Franklin: Boudreaux, Hebert, Landry, LeBlanc, Robicheaux
Baldwin: Boudreaux, Hebert, Landry, Bodin, Simoneaux
Jeanerette: Hebert, Landry, Guillotte, Broussard, LeBlanc
New Iberia: Broussard, Romero, Landry, Hebert, Viator
St. Martinville: Bienvenu, Theriot, Champagne, Broussard, Guidry
Lafayette: Broussard, Hebert, Guidry, LeBlanc, Landry
Breaux Bridge: Guidry, LeBlanc, Broussard, Hebert, Thibodeaux
Cecelia: Angelle, Calais, Guidry, Huval, LeBlanc
Arnaudville: Kidder, Olivier, Taylor, Stelly, Marks
Port Barre: Marks, Fontenot, Guillory, LeBlanc, Richard
Opelousas: Fontenot, Richard, Stelly, Pitre, Guillory
Washington: Fontenot, Soileau, Dupre, Joubert, Vidrine

More than two-thirds of the students enrolled at the University of Southwestern Louisiana, located in the Teche country, are of the Roman Catholic faith. The Catholic Student Center is in the center of the campus. It is doubtful that a similar situation exists at any other state-supported institution of higher learning in the country, except at Francis T. Nicholls State College in Thibodaux.

Not too long ago an interesting conversation was overheard on the campus at Southwestern. A petite dark-haired co-ed told another co-ed "Can you imagine? One of my professors doesn't even speak French!" The fact is, however, that a professor in Lafayette or an oil man from Texas who moves to Lafayette no longer has any need to learn French. And the boys and girls coming to the University from all over the Teche country are coming, in increasing numbers, with little knowledge of French. If they are required to study a foreign language, they may elect Spanish or German, fearing that they will be at a disadvantage in a French class—an unfounded fear usually, inasmuch as Cajun French is a spoken rather than a written language and adheres to few rules of French grammar.

It is quite probable that the French language will persist longer among the

Negroes than among the Cajuns. Visitors to the Teche country, usually prepared to overhear some French spoken by Cajuns, are quite startled to hear the Negroes speaking French. But this is changing, for Negro children as well as Cajun children are staying in school longer than ever before, and school is taught in English. Although television is accelerating the trend away from French, it is still wise for a politician campaigning on television to say a few words in French to prove that he is a "man of the people."

Because of large families and increased emphasis on education, enrollment at the University of Southwestern Louisiana is rising sharply. It is a great source of pride to a Cajun that he has "given" two of his children to the "Church" and eight to "Southwestern." Some of the wealthier families send their children to Louisiana State University in Baton Rouge. But Cajuns feel they are in a minority group there, and they tend to get homesick.

Nobody drinks stronger coffee than the Cajuns. Drunk in a small demitasse or in large cups, the flavor is not important but café noir has to be strong. Few Cajuns roast and grind their own coffee anymore, but they buy dark-roast brands manufactured in Baton Rouge, Lafayette, or Beaumont. Expensive coffee is not used, inasmuch as it is almost burnt in the roasting process. Cajun coffee, unlike "New Orleans coffee," does not contain chicory. It is almost impossible to satisfy your thirst for "decent" coffee in other places after living a few years in the Cajun country.

A favorite entertainment in the Teche country is the public dance, called the *fais-dodo*. Commonly held on Friday, Saturday, or Sunday nights, *fais-dodo*s are a highlight of every festival and are even sponsored by politicians seeking office. Another favorite of the Cajuns, horse racing, has recently gone "big time" with the completion in 1966 of a major racetrack, Evangeline Downs, north of Lafayette.

This brings us to the tendency to "stay put." Cajuns have strong family attachments. Then, too, never underestimate the power of a woman, especially a Cajun woman. It simply is not practical to encourage a Cajun to take an excellent job opportunity beyond New Orleans, Baton Rouge, or Houston, if any other job at all is available locally. For example, one graduate of the University of Southwestern Louisiana was about to take a job in Houma which is, after all, well within French Louisiana, when his wife and her family stopped it.

It may be that it is simply too disconcerting to hear such a common name as Broussard (and there are 490 listed in the Lafayette telephone directory) pronounced *Browsard* instead of *Brew-sard* or Hebert (291 in the Lafayette telephone directory) pronounced *Heebert* instead of *A-bear*. Such happens in a city as close to French Louisiana as Shreveport. If that is what keeps them down on the Teche, loveliest of southern streams, *c'est la vie*!

The Atchafalaya

By SUE LYLES EAKIN

THE ATCHAFALAYA IS A CINDERELLA RIVER which was transformed in recent times from a mere natural drainage system for the seasonal overflow waters of the Mississippi and Red rivers into a mighty river itself. For not much more than a century has this modern miracle of nature flowed with such volume to the Gulf of Mexico from its interesting beginning in central Louisiana. Until as late as the mid-1800's, the nondescript stream flowing through an almost impenetrable wilderness area was choked with debris and matted with logs, upon which vegetation flourished and further discouraged the growth of the little stream. But all that was changed after around 1831, and the amazing story of the once insignificant stream growing into a great river began.

The name, which is spelled one way and pronounced another, is a Choctaw Indian word from *hacha* meaning "river" and *falaia* meaning "long." It is pronounced "Chaff-a-li-a." René Robert Cavelier, Sieur de la Salle, and Henri (Ironhand) de Tonti saw the Atchafalaya when they explored the Mississippi to its mouth in 1679. Indian guides pointed it out, told them the strange name, but the explorers were not impressed. The Atchafalaya, after all, was really just one of an intricate network of small streams in the area then—it had a few more centuries to go before folks would take notice of it.

The Atchafalaya and the uncounted little bayous and distributaries crisscrossing each other in the Atchafalaya Basin were a headache to pioneers. The Acadian refugees deported from Nova Scotia, searching for homes in Louisiana, crossed the eastern portion of the Atchafalaya swamp. "The forest primeval" could well have referred to this land.

In a search for timber for ships following the War of 1812, the United States Navy needed live oak and red cedar for shipbuilding. An agent for the government named James Leander Cathart led an expedition which officially investigated for the first time the Atchafalaya swamplands. He left the first official reports about the stream.

The Atchafalaya begins dramatically at a confluence in central Louisiana with two other rivers—Old River, which forms a connection with the Mississippi, and Red River. Here, where the Red and the Mississippi run together, the waters shed from a large part of the North American Continent, and the full-grown Atchafalaya River emerges and gathers its own murky waters for a quick southward trip to the Gulf of Mexico. Only from the air can one catch the breathtaking panoramic view of this phenomenon.

One of the fascinating features about the Atchafalaya is that in its 145 incredibly picturesque miles to the Gulf it achieves the same distance that the Mississippi River takes 322 miles to span—a shortcut representing a saving of 177 miles for the trip. This shorter route to the Gulf presents a chilling threat that, under flood conditions of the future, the gigantic Mississippi itself might forsake its own meandering course and take over that of the Atchafalaya. Such an appalling eventuality would leave Baton Rouge and New Orleans stranded on marshy lagoons. And, presumably, the Mississippi, like Cinderella's stepsister, would find the relatively small channel of the Atchafalaya too confining. Then, some speculate, its waters would burst through the Atchafalaya Basin, inundating 1,300 square miles of farmland and forests through which the Atchafalaya now flows.

So real is this threat of the Atchafalaya that for nearly four decades a historic controversy has raged over proposals of the United States Army Corps of Engineers to prevent such a catastrophe as the changing of the Mississippi's flow from its own channel—and the taking over of that of the Atchafalaya—a proposition of such momentous proportions that few men can comprehend its implications.

The Atchafalaya has not always been of such importance. Its location on the west bank of the Mississippi made it a trap for all the debris floating down the river. A mat of logs eventually covered the little stream, and it was not until 1831, when Captain Henry Miller Shreve negotiated his famous "cutoff" straightening the course of the Mississippi, that the debris was cleared away. Some of this was being done as late as 1875. With the unexpected aid of extraordinary flood conditions, the lowly little stream suddenly swelled into the proportions of a great river. What is more, it was discovered by appalled observers that the volume of the stream was increasing year by year—from diversion of waters of the Mississippi flowing into Old River and then into the Atchafalaya.

After the disastrous 1927 flood, measures were taken by the Federal Government to forestall any possibility of such a calamity occurring again. Vast sums were allocated under the Flood Control Act of 1928. Significant among the major features of this bill was the erection of a system of locks and navigation channels to regulate and control the flow of the Mississippi waters into Old River. It would control firmly the Atchafalaya's source of water draining from the Mississippi, limiting this flow to about 25 percent in normal times.

As if this attention were not enough for a lowly-born drainage channel that turned into a great river, the Atchafalaya has captured outraged public attention for another reason. The Atchafalaya flows through an area incomparable for its undisturbed wilderness, an area more precious than the famous Okefenokee Swamp of Georgia, an area laced with countless streams and lakes and alive with wildlife. The atomic-age flood-control plans would wreck one of the last surviving wilderness areas in the world, the sportsmen say; and already the locks have prevented the age-old business of drying and flooding of the streams which added the final boon for wildlife in the Atchafalaya Basin.

What is more, some critics of the flood-control plan say that the plans of the Corps of Engineers will open new sections of the swamp to settlement as flooding ceases, population increases, and the need for new farmland multiplies.

So the majestic river flows on to the Coast, flanked now by a complex of floodways—the West Atchafalaya, the Atchafalaya Basin, and Morganza floodways enclosing an area about seventeen miles wide and seventy-five miles long at the northern part of the river.

Rivers—like houses, as a poet noted—"take a heap of livin' " to make a living thing, and the Atchafalaya has seen a lot of living. That is why, quivering there in the sun, resting there in the twilight, the Atchafalaya is different from all other rivers to those who know it best. It is as though the river is a breathing thing. The joy of a calliope; the thrill of a good catch; the sweet weariness after a hard day's work on a river; the refreshing feel of a stolen swim; the hates and loves and gladness and misery of everyday living; the satisfaction of knowing that, whatever else changes, some things, like rivers, go on forever—of all these the Atchafalaya has become a part to those who know and love it best.

No big city—not even a medium-sized city—marks the meeting of the Big Three rivers in central Louisiana. There is a small town drowsing there by the waters—Simmesport, a sawmill town, center of small farms and cattle lands, and a fishermen's town. For wherever the Atchafalaya flows—from Simmesport to Morgan City—people and towns along its banks share its largess of fish. Simmesport fishermen make their living on the sale of catfish, gaspergou, buffalo, and garfish caught in the Atchafalaya. Their proud claim is that there is no catfish like the 'Chafalaya cat—the blue or channel cat, the yellow or Opelousas cat, and the lesser known spoonbill cat. In a history of Avoyelles Parish towns, the author mentions the politician of Simmesport who was described as having more fishing boats on the Atchafalaya than George VI had ships on the Atlantic.

At Simmesport every local schoolboy has heard the stories of the Civil War, of when Union soldiers advanced into central Louisiana by transport up the Atchafalaya and many a skirmish was fought in the area. Most marvelous to relate, however, is the story of the Union crossing of the Atchafalaya as the Union army retreated (as they say in Simmesport) from Federal General Nathaniel P. Banks's famous Red River Campaign of 1864. It was here that the remarkable Westerner, Colonel Joseph Bailey, who fashioned the dam at Alexandria to save the Yankee fleet from extermination, was forced to call upon all of his ingenuity and engineering genius to get the Yanks back across the Atchafalaya. Schoolboys do not need to be content with only the half-believed stories of the oldtimers about Civil War glory here on the Atchafalaya. History books are studded with pictures in black and white, for all the world to see, of how Colonel Bailey assembled and constructed a pontoon bridge of transports anchored and lashed four abreast, connected them with gangplanks and boards, and, forming a continuous roadway, allowed the Union troops, their horses and artillery, and the wagon trains to move across.

After loading all of the wounded and sick and exhausted aboard the transports, history takes note, the entire fleet steamed toward the Mississippi River while the army marched overland to Morganza. One Connecticut soldier wrote in his memoirs: "At one o'clock we moved across the Atchafalaya on a magnificent bridge, of twenty large steamboats, lying side by side. Another such bridge this country has rarely if ever seen."

Simmesport lads may not only admire the ingenuity of an extraordinary Yankee engineer, but the unquenchable southern pride rises again when the story is retold. For, as local historians have it, if the Union forces had not negotiated the Atchafalaya at this moment with such dispatch, the Johnny Rebs would have captured them all—and possibly won the war.

From south Louisiana near the Gulf to central Louisiana, the Atchafalaya was the scene of a lot of excitement during the Civil War. At Morgan City (Brashear City) the area was alive with Union forces preparing to march into Louisiana in the famous river campaign. Camp Lovell, at the southern end of the river, was designed to serve as an advanced-training center and to man Fort Berwick, which guarded the inlet from Berwick Bay into the Atchafalaya. Steamboats, both Union and Confederate, plied the waters of the Atchafalaya. Skirmishes were fought along its banks, and troops camped alongside the river here and there from central Louisiana to the Gulf.

A few miles farther downstream from Simmesport, on the way to the Gulf, the broadening Atchafalaya is enlivened with attention it draws from another town on its banks, Melville. Melville and the Atchafalaya are inseparable. Oldtimers are full of the lore of the story of the river—the time the railroad bridge was built over it in '83 (or was it '84?), the quaint boats

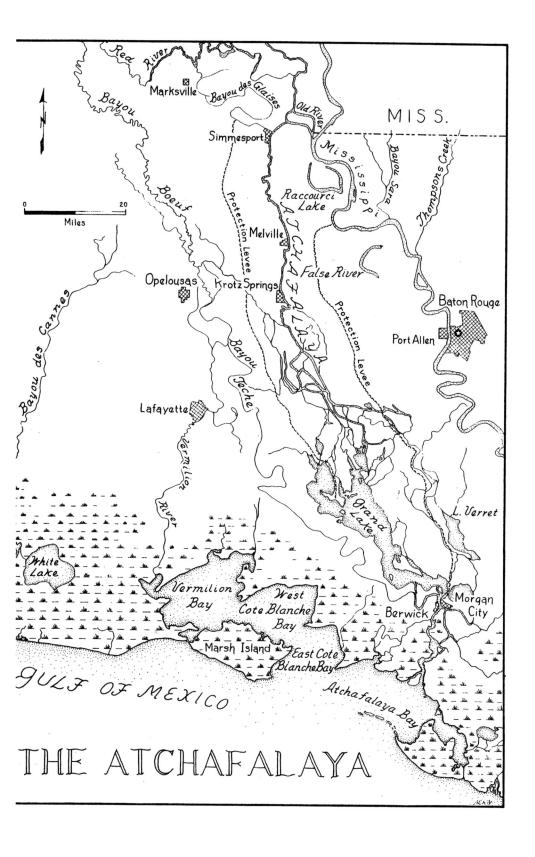

the oldtimers used, the flood of 1912 which was practically nothing, it turned out later, compared to the devastation of 1927.

An elderly woman reminisced about Melville and the Atchafalaya nearly a century ago. "This," she said, indicating the heart of Melville, "was all woods and marsh and full of sloughs and bayous. The stores that were here were along the levee, and the levee wasn't any more than a potato ridge, about so high. The Atchafalaya was little, like a bayou, then, and when it rose, the water went out in sloughs and bayous.

"There were flathouses floating in the river then and my uncle owned one of them. He sold tobacco and stuff like that. . . . I remember . . . the stores along the river front. There were walks along the levee to go into the stores. . . ."

Fish! fish! fish! As at Simmesport, fishing is a way of living at Melville. Oldtimers recall that at the turn of the century there were five or six fish docks; in 1896, the train stopped to load fish for shipment to Texas. There were fishing boats and boats for transporting the fish to market in New Orleans.

A native paints a nostalgic picture of the days before more modern transportation replaced the river as the inland town's chief artery for communication with the world outside: "Showboats docked here about once a year. There were two of them—French and Robertson's, and one had two boats. One of the boats carried animals that were penned like in a zoo. I saw my first silent movie on French's showboat back in '98 or '99.

"When the showboats were coming, you could hear the calliope playing 'way 'round the bend and we children would line up on the levee to see the showboat come up. Everybody went; there was nothing else to do, and we waited for those boats to come!

"The showboat that carried the animals had elephants and lions and everything! The glamour from childhood remains for oldtimers thinking of the Atchafalaya and the way it shaped their lives."

At Krotz Springs, a filling station operator speaks for the river's meaning to another generation grown up on its banks. The young fellow speaks of the river as a man might his wife. "That river," he says affectionately.

He speaks a little sadly. "Fishing? It ain't what it used to be before them locks. We still catch catfish and crappie and gous, of course, but it ain't like it used to be. . . . We got a port here. . . . Wish I had a silver dime for every hour of fun I've had swimming in the old river!"

One feature that makes the future of the Atchafalaya River and its basin a matter of interest to the nation's conservationists is the presence of its awe-inspiring wilderness area. Here in unbelievable pristine beauty are seemingly endless miles of untouched wilds which can never be replaced. Birds, insects, and wild animals break the silence of a strange world—half land, half water—where hoary, age-old trees shade uncounted quiet streams. Here birds in this world of the Atchafalaya flit from leaf to trembling leaf in the perpetual dusk of a swampland screened by moss-hung trees and mirrored in still, small lakes. This picturesque bit of river land affords that rare glimpse of forests untouched by man, this continent before its European conquerors set foot here. Its sight stirs in every man an unexplained wistfulness for a glimpse of the world before time began—and around the Atchafalaya, perhaps, it lies as near that mystery of the ages as anywhere on the globe.

Amazingly enough, a visitor may find a road atop a levee which roughly parallels the Atchafalaya River, stretching from west of Krotz Springs to the southern termination near Charenton. From the comfort of an automobile, he can catch the flavor and enjoy the many-faceted beauty of this wilderness paradise. It is an anachronism in this age, when trips to the moon are given priority, to find that such a place still exists.

The Atchafalaya is the fishermen's Eden. All the freshwater fish of warm southern waters gambol here—largemouth and spotted bass, black and white crappie, white and yellow bass, many species of bream, and catfish. Whether for sport or for a living, fishing and the Atchafalaya are synonymous. The number of sport fishermen who enjoy the Atchafalaya and its labryinth of lakes and streams within the basin was checked in May, 1963, by the Louisiana Wild Life and Fisheries Commission. In nine days there were 17,990 fishermen, who caught 200,168 fish during the period. These figures are even more impressive when another fact is added—most of the Atchafalaya Basin was not even considered in the survey!

Boating on the Atchafalaya itself and in the maze of countless waterways within the basin is a dreamy experience. As for hunting, the sky over the river has often been black with ducks, for the pattern of dewatering and flooding was made for waterfowl. Squirrels, deer, bear, and rabbits, panthers, alligators, and snakes live in the Atchafalaya wonderland. Bullfrogs, crawfish, and turtles offer their special contributions. Tasty delicacies that they are, they add the lure of "something different" to the Atchafalaya variety of sports. Production of crawfish in the basin is a new million-dollar industry.

Trappers early found that the area was right for fur-bearing animals, and in more recent years nutria have been added to the list of animals worthwhile for the trapper. Muskrat, mink, raccoon, otter, and opossum are the principal fur-bearing animals around the Cinderella river.

During the past decades this land of primitive beauty has been tapped for oil, and the "chug-chug-chug" from the wells, the twinkle of lights on oil derricks, the ridiculous gait of marsh buggies, the busy whir of helicopter propellers, dredges, barges, and airplanes with pontoons have all been added to the life along the lower Atchafalaya.

The Atchafalaya's fabulous area, of course, contains riches in timber. Cypress, cedar, oak—name them—they are there in the thick growth bordering the river.

The Atchafalaya claims two cosmopolitan coastal towns, Morgan City and Berwick. Here, in contrast to the area of small towns around Simmesport or the plantations along its way or the fabulous wilderness area, is the growing city, smelling of salt air from the Gulf, its fishing boats at the dock, its fishnets in the sun to dry, busy men freezing, canning, selling fish. The fishing town to end all fishing towns . . . fish . . . boats . . . oil . . . timber. . . . Morgan City includes in its romance a location on the Old Spanish Trail (US 90), which crosses the Atchafalaya on a splendid steel bridge. Engineers found themselves with an unusual problem here because of the great depth of the Atchafalaya at this point. It was necessary to rest one of the piers on the deepest foundation in the world, 176 feet below the low-water stage. This is, perhaps, the reason for the widespread belief among Louisianians that the Atchafalaya is the deepest river in the world.

The Atchafalaya for all its identification as the heart of a primeval wilderness area is in touch with the space age. Between 1947 and 1956, traffic on the Atchafalaya River increased 1,801 percent, according to a report by the American Waterways Operators, Incorporated. With 121 miles of navigable waterway between Simmesport and Morgan City, the Atchafalaya traffic has been phenomenal. The river's role in modern commerce has been sparked by heavy increases in shipment of petroleum and petroleum products. The astounding change in tonnage from 1947 to 1956 was from 194,257 net tons to 3,694,530. Figuring largely in this commerce is the thirty-mile route from Morgan City to the Gulf of Mexico which, during those same years, showed an increase of 250 percent in net tonnage. Its importance is enhanced by the fact that it is crossed by the intracoastal canal.

The Atchafalaya, in a final flourish as it sweeps into the Gulf, broadens out to form beautiful Grand Lake. It is at a narrow point of the lake that the river ends its trip to the sea.

Murky-brown, tufted on its banks by a skyline of trees, the Atchafalaya, every inch the inexplicable force great rivers become, flows imperturbably on out to sea.

Bayou Lafourche

By PHILIP D. UZEE

THE TRAVELER ALONG LOUISIANA HIGHWAY ONE—following the west bank of Bayou Lafourche from Donaldsonville in Ascension Parish, past Napoleonville in Assumption Parish, through Thibodaux to Leeville in Lafourche Parish—will find himself in an area as modern as the mid-1960's with a history dating back to the late 1690's. He will note that both the rural and urban sections are provided with electric power, natural or butane gas, and a constant supply of fresh water. He will go through busy cities and towns, complete with modern shopping centers and clusters of subdivisions. He will speed by mechanized farms and plantations, all fronting on the bayou, and notice in the background an occasional sugar mill or refinery. He will pass new and old churches with their neighboring cemeteries of aboveground tombs, modern school buildings, Francis T. Nicholls State College in Thibodaux, and well-equipped public and private hospitals.

Along the highway, the traveler will see pre-Civil War mansions, such as "Belle Alliance," "Madewood," and "Rienzi," as well as modern ranch houses, split-levels, and colonials intermingled with old-time Acadian cottages, most of them having a television antenna showing above the roof line and many with two cars in the carport. When he reaches Cut Off, he will note that the buildings are closer together; Galliano and Golden Meadow are as congested as large cities because the amount of solid land near the bayou is limited, and there is very little living space and farmland. Lower Lafourche is the domain of the fisherman with his seagoing luggers equipped with the latest electronic devices, of seafood preparation factories, of workers engaged in the business of exploring, drilling, and extracting petroleum from both inshore and offshore fields. Upon completing his tour, the traveler will conclude that the people along Bayou Lafourche live the good life and that here everything is up to date.

Amid the hustle and bustle, the bayou flows from the Mississippi River for a distance of 110 miles to the Gulf of Mexico. From Donaldsonville to Lockport, it meanders like a natural canal between green-lined banks. From Lockport to the Fourchon (the mouth of the bayou), it is one of the busiest waterways in South Louisiana. The traffic is generated by the Intracoastal Canal—the main inland waterway connecting Brownsville, Texas, with Appalachicola, Florida—which joins the bayou at Lockport and Larose, and by the oil and fishing industries which use water transportation. The lower part of the bayou promises to be even busier in the future, for a multimillion-dollar port development is under construction at the Fourchon.

It was not at the Fourchon that Bayou Lafourche came into the ken of recorded history, but at its source, the Mississippi River. The French-Canadian explorer Pierre Le Moyne, Sieur d'Iberville, on his first voyage up the Mississippi in 1699 noted the stream which formed a fork with the river at thirty degrees, seven minutes, north latitude and ninety-one degrees west longitude. Iberville made contact with the Washa Indians who lived on its banks. Jean Baptiste Le Moyne, Sieur de Bienville, Iberville's brother, sailed down the stream and explored it for a distance of about thirty miles in September, 1699. Around 1706, the warlike Chitimacha tribe moved in large numbers from the Grand Lake area to settle along the upper portions of the bayou. The French had many altercations with this tribe, and the colonial authorities referred to their tribal lands as being located on the Bayou Lafourche (French for "fork") of the Chetimachas. After the United States acquired Louisiana, the name was shortened to "Bayou Lafourche."

The area was not developed or settled to any extent during the French period. In the 1760's, the Spanish, who were in possession of Louisiana, permitted the Acadians, who had been expelled from their homes in Canada, to settle along the Mississippi in a region that is now St. James and Ascension parishes. Attracted by the fertile soil, some of the Acadians settled the lands along the bayou which were nearest the river. In 1772, the Spanish established the ecclesiastical parish of Ascension at the Lafourche of the Chetimachas. In 1778, the district of Valenzuela was established to encompass the present Assumption Parish.

By 1806, the population of the Lafourche country was 3,533; and all the lands fronting on Bayou Lafourche for a distance of eighty-three miles from the river had been granted by the Spanish government to Acadians (Boudreauxs, Heberts, Robicheauxs, Theriots, Bergerons); Spaniards from the Canary Islands (Hernandezes, Martinezes, Hidalgos, Truxillos); and Germans who had migrated from the German Coast of the Mississippi (Toupses, Folses, Triches, Trosclairs). The influx of Americans (Pughs, Nichollses, Martins, Kitteridges, Whites, Bowies) came in the 1820's. Actual settlement was confined to the area nearest the river. By the 1830's, the area of settlement extended as far down the bayou as Lockport. In the 1850's, the Larose-

Cut Off section was inhabited; and, in the 1870's, the Cheramies began settling the Golden Meadow area.

The culture and mores of the Latin-Catholic pioneers became dominant in the Lafourche country. Newcomers generally conform to the pattern of *la vie Lafourchaise*. Although the French-Acadian language is spoken still in all parts of the area, more and more of its people speak only English. The principal feast days of the Catholic church are observed as legal holidays; restaurants feature meatless menus on Friday. Each community has its Mardi Gras festivities which include, in most cases, balls and parades.

On their march down the bayou the pioneers established farms, side by side, fronting the stream. The average farm was six arpents front by forty arpents deep (one arpent equals 192 feet). This was the fertile highland nearest the bayou. Beyond the forty-arpent line were occasional ridges, or *Brules,* trembling prairies, or the swamps. The *petit habitant* grew corn, cotton, rice, and vegetables on his farm. His good wife wove a blue cottonade cloth from cotton to make the clothes for the family. From 1803 to 1820, the Lafourche country was the domain of the small farmer. After 1820, Americans (Anglo-Saxon Protestants) came in increasing numbers. They established sugarcane plantations, in many cases buying out the small farmers who retreated farther down the bayou or to the *Brules,* brought in Negro slaves, built mills and refineries. In 1840, sugarcane was the leading crop on Bayou Lafourche. The social and economic pattern set by the planters was to endure through the Civil War and on into the early part of the twentieth century.

Planters, *petits habitants,* businessmen, all depended on the bayou as their main artery of communications and transportation; the steamboat was the most important watercraft plying its waters. The first steamboat on the bayou appeared in the 1820's and was commanded by Captain F. N. Streck, an almost legendary figure who had operated a schooner on the bayou before the advent of the steamboat. From January to June, when the bayou was high, large river steamboats could enter it; small boats could operate only from December to August. When no steamboats could navigate the bayou due to low water, heavy freight was moved on towboats pulled by towlines (*cordelles*) attached to mules or horses that plodded along paths on top of the levee. Steamboats took two days to make the trip to New Orleans and two days to return. In the 1840's, flatboats from the Midwest came to Bayou Lafourche with beef, pork, corn, oats, and fruit to exchange for sugar and molasses.

The wants of the bayou folk which could not be met on the farm were supplied by trading boats (*caboteurs*). There were oyster, fish, and fruit boats; ice boats, restaurant and saloon boats; showboats, photograph boats; and boats with doctors and dentists. Soon after the turn of the century, the trading boats were supplanted by peddling wagons which brought the merchandise needed by the housewife to her front gate. The wagons were supplanted by the "rolling stores," which in turn have largely been supplanted by the supermarket.

To get from one side of the bayou to the other, flatboats, pirogues, and ferries were used. Only a few bridges had been constructed by the turn of the century. There was a ferry in front of every church and school, as well as at the principal crossing in each community. The latter was usually a toll ferry leased by the police jury to the person who was the highest bidder for the privilege of operating the ferry in the community.

Since the bayou was a distributary of the Mississippi, the level of the water depended on the level of the river. During the high-water season on the Mississippi, the bayous could become a raging torrent. This necessitated the construction of levees to guard against floods. The original levees were built and maintained by the property owners. Sometimes the levee could not stand the strain of the eroding water and a break, or crevasse, would occur, putting many acres of land underwater. In the latter part of the nineteenth century, a movement was started to build locks at the "fork" at Donaldsonville to control the flow of water into the bayou. The movement culminated in the damming of the bayou at its source in 1904. The locks were never built. Bayou Lafourche, from Donaldsonville to Lockport, became a still, lifeless stream, choked with water hyacinths (locally known as water lilies) from bank to bank. The levees, which were no longer needed, were cut down in many places, and the batture was used to plant vegetable gardens and for homesites.

Under the auspices of the Bayou Lafourche Water District, a pumping station was put into operation at Donaldsonville in 1955. Once again Mississippi River water flows in Bayou Lafourche, supplying fresh water to residents and industry, and the hyacinths are gone. Fishing and swimming in the bayou were once favorite forms of recreation for the people, but the bayou was stagnant for so long that Lafourchians had to find other fishing spots and swimming places. Today, boating and water-skiing are the only water sports enjoyed on the bayou.

Dancing has always been a favorite amusement. In former times a family invited its neighbors to a *bal ce soir* by firing a gun. Dancing partners were selected by drawing from two packs of cards. A fiddle and an accordian provided the music. Then came the era of the jitney dance. Each community had a dance pavilion, usually built on the bayou side, operated as a profit-making venture by an individual. Everyone in the community and its immediate surroundings went to the dance on Saturday night. The young adults came to dance and to court; the children to play; the babies

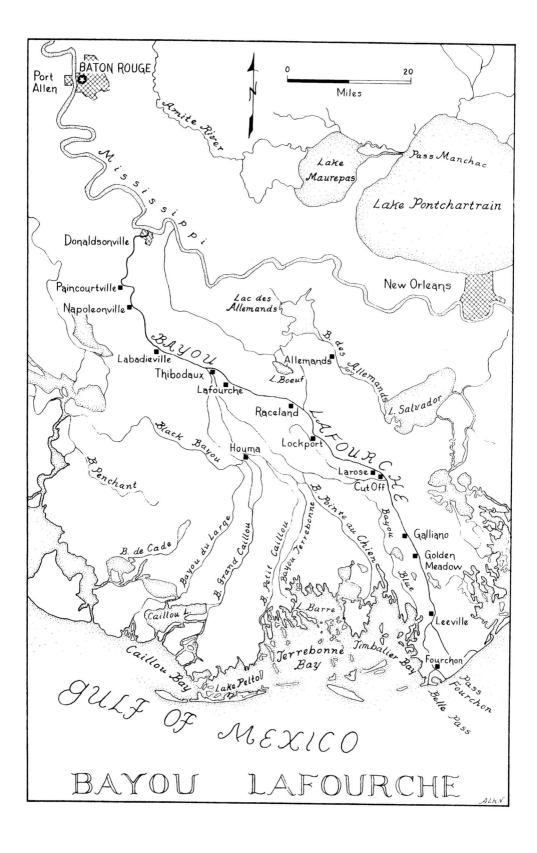

to sleep (*fais-dodo*); the mothers and grandmothers to sit on benches around the dance floor to gossip, chaperone, and keep time with the music with a palmetto fan; the fathers and grandfathers to drink and talk at the bar or to play *bourré,* pedro, or poker in the game room. No newly married couple considered themselves properly wed unless they had a *bal de noce* at the community dance hall. Today the pavilions that remain have been converted into nightclubs, which do not provide family entertainment.

The favorite spectator sport after the turn of the century was baseball. Each town had its team made up of local men, and the ball parks were crowded every Sunday afternoon during the season. Rivalry between towns was intense, and sometimes games had to be called because of a free-for-all involving not only the players but the spectators. Today, this fierce community pride and loyalty is lavished on the high-school football team. The automobile, World War II, and television have changed many things, *mon ami!*

It has not been all fun along the bayou. Yellow-fever epidemics, with their quarantines and patrols, floods, and hurricanes have been experienced by the people, who have been resilient enough to take them in stride. They buried the dead and rebuilt shattered lives and property. In 1893, a hurricane destroyed Cheniere Caminada. The survivors moved inland to establish Leeville, which was destroyed by a hurricane in 1915. The survivors moved to Golden Meadow. Leeville remained a wasteland until 1931, when the first of hundreds of producing oil wells and gas wells were brought in. The marsh there came to resemble a veritable forest of oil derricks. Hurricane Betsy, the worst in memory, packing 150-mile-an-hour winds, struck the bayou country in 1965, leaving millions of dollars in destroyed property in its wake, including the oil derricks at Leeville. Once again, the region recovered from disaster to resume its pre-Betsy daily routine.

The Lafourche country, because of its wealth and its proximity to New Orleans, became a target for an invading Federal army in 1862. Donaldsonville was bombarded by Federal gunboats on the Mississippi. Major engagements were fought at Kock's Plantation, Georgia Landing (Labadieville), and Lafourche Crossing. For most of the Civil War years, the region was occupied by Federal forces and was considered a part of Federal Louisiana. The Lafourche country emerged from the war poverty-stricken but proud of its contribution to the Confederate cause, counting among its heroes Francis T. Nicholls, future governor and State supreme court justice; Leonidas Polk, "the Fighting Bishop of the Confederacy," who owned "Leighton" plantation near Thibodaux and founded the Episcopal churches in the area; and General Braxton Bragg. Edward Douglass White, a native of Lafourche who became Chief Justice of the United States Supreme Court, was in Port

Hudson when it was besieged by the Federal forces and was made a prisoner when the position was surrendered.

Lafourche men have responded to the call to arms since the expeditions of Spanish Governor Bernardo de Gálvez against the British in the Floridas during the American Revolution. They fought in the Battle of New Orleans, the Spanish-American War, the two World Wars, the Korean War, and Vietnam. Many have made the supreme sacrifice, and their names are inscribed on public monuments and in the churches of their community.

The region boasts of its saints as well as of its heroes. Near Donaldsonville is the shrine of St. Amico, who appeared as a dark young stranger at the home of young Lucien Musco in 1906 to cure him of an apparently fatal fever. Lucien's father, in gratitude, built a small chapel about ten feet square to house a statue of the saint which had been imported from Italy. An annual celebration honoring St. Amico is held the Sunday after Easter. A procession, led by the statue borne on the shoulders of an honor guard, wends its way from the shrine to the Church of the Ascension in Donaldsonville. Many of the marchers are barefooted. After the religious services, feasting and dancing are enjoyed.

St. Valerie is the special protectress honored by the people of Thibodaux. She was a second-century Christian martyr whose authenticated relic was brought to St. Joseph's church in 1868 by Father Charles M. Menard, who was pastor from 1845 to 1899. An altar was dedicated to her honor, and the relic was placed in an elaborate reliquary made in Holland. Her feast day was celebrated on April 28, and the relic was carried in procession, with the young ladies of the Confraternity of St. Valerie forming the guard of honor. In 1916, the church in which the relic was kept was destroyed by fire, but St. Valerie was saved and the reliquary is in the present St. Joseph's church. The altar and the Confraternity are no more, but St. Valerie is still invoked in times of danger, such as hurricanes, to intercede for Thibodaux.

An almost continuous community stretches from Donaldsonville to Golden Meadow on both sides of Bayou Lafourche. For this reason the people are said to live on "the Longest Street in America." Although the community is made up of diverse parts, the historic stream acts as a unifying force. Places are located up the bayou, down the bayou, or across the bayou. As the inhabitants go about their daily routine or speed along the twin highways which parallel the bayou, they are unconsciously aware of its presence; it is always there and has always been there.

An extension of the way of life on Bayou Lafourche is found along the bayous of Terrebonne Parish. Before 1822, Lafourche and Terrebonne parishes comprised the parish of Lafourche Interior. The area contains many bayous. The principal ones are Terrebonne, Black, Blue, du Large, Petit Calliou, and Grand Calliou. The Terrebonne bayous flow through fertile sugar farms and plantations to a wilderness of tidal marshes and lagoons.

The same ethnic groups which populated Bayou Lafourche inhabited the banks of Terrebonne's bayous in the "line-village" pattern of settlement. The Americans established their sugar plantations on Bayous Terrebonne and Black and on Little Bayou Black. The Acadians, French, Germans, and Spanish settled on all the bayous.

The hub of the parish is Houma on Bayou Terrebonne. It is a busy city: the political, economic, and cultural capital of an area rich in agricultural, mineral, and human resources. All the highways and waterways lead to Houma, which was named for an Indian tribe that inhabited the area.

The people of Terrebonne are a progressive people with a deep pride in the cultural heritage which they share with their cousins on Bayou Lafourche.

Oil Barge on Lower Bayou Teche

New Iberia Chamber of Commerce

Office of Secretary of State

"The Shadows," New Iberia

Louisiana Department of Commerce and Industry

Blessing of the Shrimp Fleet, Morgan City

Louisiana Department of Commerce and Industry
Trappers, Lower Atchafalaya

Louisiana Department of Commerce and Industry

The Trapper, Coastal Marshes Along the Lower Atchafalaya

Thibodaux Chamber of Commerce

Oil Rig, Bayou Lafourche

Louisiana Department of Commerce and Industry
Icing a Trawler, Lower Bayou Lafourche

Louisiana Department of Commerce and Industry

Bayou Lafourche at Golden Meadow

Old-time Oyster Bar, Bayou Lafourche

Oyster Shells, Lower Bayou Lafourche

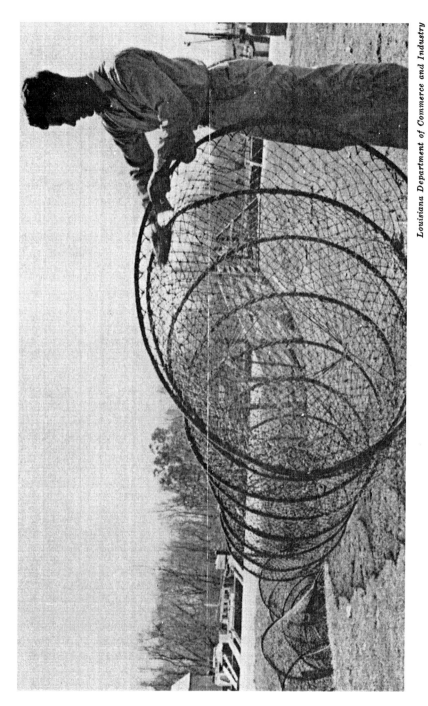

Commercial Fishing Trap, Lower Bayou Lafourche

Louisiana Department of Commerce and Industry

"Rienzi," Near Thibodaux

Louisiana Tourist Development Commission

Part V | *Southeast Louisiana*

The Lower Mississippi

By JOSEPH G. TREGLE, JR.

ASK A NEW ORLEANIAN TODAY which is his favorite spot along the Coast, and he will doubtless begin to regale you with a listing of the particular attractions of Biloxi, Bay St. Louis, Santa Rosa Island, or yet another of the famed resort playgrounds along the Gulf of Mexico east of Pearl River. A reply by his ancestor of a hundred or more years ago would have made no such jump to distant shores, for to him the "Coast" was only one thing, and it was right at his doorstep—the twisting, sinuous banks of the Mississippi from beyond Baton Rouge down to the sea.

From the earliest days of Louisiana as a French and Spanish colony this had been the spinal column from which depended the region's settlement and growth, as it is in large part even today. And always its vital substance has been the Mississippi, wrapping within itself the discharge of countless thousands of miles of great tributaries which themselves vein even more countless acres of the heartland of America.

There is more than one Mississippi, of course, even to the Louisianians along the Coast, for no single visage, no one mood or personality could accommodate the protean capacities of a phenomenon created by such awesome forces as those which gave the river birth in distant ages of geological time. From Lake Itasca to St. Paul and Minneapolis, it roams through a broad old valley, falls then into the steeply palisaded trench stretching down to Cairo, and from here moves into the loess-hill, clay-bluff terrain which it built eons ago with the richness of its deposits. This, too, is left behind as the Mississippi rolls past Baton Rouge into the youngest of its channels, through the flat alluvial plain pushing to the Gulf. Just above Baton Rouge near Poplar Grove deep water begins, really deep water, where Samuel Clemens once claimed that the river went down 200 feet. Today its depth in this last stretch to the sea may range from 50 feet to 100 feet on an average, sufficient to allow oceangoing vessels to navigate up to the docks of Baton Rouge.

But this deepwater Mississippi concedes no more to regularity or sameness than it is willing to support upstream. From Baton Rouge to New Orleans its run is through a fairly wide plain, stretching for several miles behind either levee, where the fertility of the soil once gave life to a continuous row of sugar plantations reaching down to the Crescent City through the Acadian and German Coasts, sections populated even today by the descendants of the tragic Canadian exiles and John Law's exploited adventurers from Europe. Sugarcane is still grown here, of course, though the proud old mansions of antebellum days have almost all, one by one, gone up in flames, slowly slipped into the waters of the aberrant river, or simply succumbed to the decay of neglect and hardship. Some yet remain, none more beautiful than "Oak Alley" on the west bank below Donaldsonville, reminiscent of the days when the Aimses, the Romans, the Tristes, and the Bringiers set the social and political tone along these shores.

Not far below Donaldsonville, at Manresa on the east bank, stands another memento of the Coast's opulence and of its determination to shield its own values, the magnificent white-columned structure which now serves as a Jesuit retreat house, but which began as Jefferson College to educate sons of planters who knew too well the enticements of the vice of New Orleans and the even greater menace of alien training hostile to the region's "peculiar institution." Just above New Orleans there are still other, older remnants of vanished glory, in colonial homes now restored by loving and vigilant owners and proudly displayed in spring tours along the oak-lined River Road.

Graceful, beautiful, treasurable, these are the nostalgic reminders of the past. Today the Coast from Baton Rouge to New Orleans, blessed with access to huge quantities of precious water and with clear access to the sea, has become more a Ruhr where once it was a Nile. Here have sprung up the massive installations of modern industry—oil refineries, bauxite and aluminum plants, complexes for converting cottonseed and bagasse, and countless other varieties of contemporary production.

New Orleans, too, has felt the industrial boom, while continuing to hold to its position as second port of the nation. Now, as in the 1830's and 1850's, the harbor is one of the staggering maritime sights of the world, with ships lined along miles of wharf space, unloading exotic goods from Latin America, feeding from the largest grain elevators in existence, or serving the booming petrochemical industries of the adjacent region. Complementing the river facilities themselves are the installations along the Industrial Canal linking the Mississippi to Lake Pontchartrain, while slightly to the east runs the newly opened deepwater outlet to the Gulf, a man-made remonstrance against the vagaries and perversity of the willful Mississippi.

Unabashed, the river continues on below New Orleans into the last of its many worlds, the deep delta. Now the land begins to narrow, shaping the remainder of the plain like the pointed end of an inverted pyramid. As it has in the miles above, the river here piles the land highest along its own banks, the so-called "front lands," which drop off rapidly to descend into "backlands," which gradually yield to marsh and quickly merge with the sea. Thus water menaces this area from front and rear, so that the delta must guard itself with levees to keep out the sea as well as the river. Water threatens constantly even in the terrain between the river and marsh levees, so uncommitted to solidity is the land, and wherever one goes there is the inescapable "chug-chug" sound of the motor pumps spitting out the excess to the swamp. The closer one comes to the Gulf the more shallow grows the depth of solid ground behind the river levees, until finally even the distinction between front land and marsh is lost and everything becomes a narrow projection of "trembling earth" jutting into the sea. Venice on the west bank and Pointe à la Hache on the east mark the farthest reach to which man has been able to push settlement tied by land communication to the regions above. To go further one must take to the water, either in boats or in the ingenious "swamp buggies" built to flit on top of the marsh.

Beyond lies a world of unique cast, where at last one can see the Mississippi actually engaged in its never ending task of building a domain through which to flow. In these farthest reaches of the delta there are few trees, for even the beautiful willow, ubiquitous elsewhere along the whole course of the river, can find here no soil substantial enough to hold its roots. There is only the endless expanse of waving and bending roseau cane, the tall, plumed reeds through which the black-tailed grackles dart and screech. All that the eye can see is this empire of mud, too recently spewed from the maw of the river to support huts or the foot of man. On occasion this "trembling earth" will give a terrifying heave, casting up huge "mud lumps" of soil from its depths, sometimes to a height of nine feet or more, which dry out into creviced and gas-exuding wens on the face of the morass. Such is the effect of the enormous weight of the river sediment as it pushes down into the yielding clay below, which leaps protestingly to the surface far above. Eventually one comes to the head of the passes, from which point the impatient river sends out a network of channels to the Gulf.

What is inhospitable to man gives profligate sustenance to other forms of life. The whole area swarms with it. Gone may be the redolent willow, the cypress, sycamore, and cottonwood of the higher river, but here the roseau cane is everywhere, filled with the sound of the white-bellied laughing gulls off to follow the food-dropping ships as far upstream as Baton Rouge. Swarming in amongst them are the slate-colored coots, the black broad-winged vultures, marsh hawks, sandpipers, plovers, *poules d'eau*, canvasbacks, stilts, and avocets. White royal terns flash their red beaks and ebony caps, while black skimmers, barking like hounds, race past to scoop up microscopic food from the laden waters. Sadly absent from their midst is the brown pelican who, like many of them, was wont to breed in the off-coast islands such as the Chandeleurs, Battledore, Breton, and Hog. Recurrent hurricanes have in recent years swept the females' eggs to sea, and now these odd-looking creatures have become strangers to the delta lands.

Little, apparently, can disturb the denizens of the underwater world, for here are still to be found the celebrated Mississippi catfish and his pseudo-relative, the spoonbill catfish or paddlefish, a literal remnant of the evolutionary past, with his sharklike snout and virtually boneless, though succulent, body. Here, too, are bass, which the natives insist on calling "gaspergou," the wrist-severing snapping turtle, the somnolent alligator, and the ferocious alligator gar, equipped for his deadly purposes with heavy armor and a jaw studded with spikelike teeth. Their kind have been here as long as man has recorded his adventures with the river.

No one can say with certainty when the first European came to the lower Mississippi—Alonso Alvarez de Pineda in 1519, Pánfilo de Narváez in the 1530's, perhaps, but this is more than a little doubtful. Certainly Hernando de Soto's lieutenant, Luis de Moscoso, and his men were here, borne to the Gulf on the waters of the Mississippi in desperate flight from implacable pursuing Indians. Pioneer for France was René Robert Cavalier, Sieur de la Salle who, on April 9, 1682, planted his standard at the head of the passes, took possession for Louis XIV, christened the land "Louisiana," and called the river the "Colbert," after Louis's great minister of finance. Others before La Salle had tried to name the mighty stream—De Soto's Spaniards had dubbed it the "Rio Grande," Father Jacques Marquette, the "Immaculate Conception"—and some were eventually to give it the name of La Salle himself. Fittingly enough, it was the Indians who would, at least in this, prevail. As La Salle noted in one of his letters, the Ojibway called the river the "Mississipy," his spelling of their *Michi Sepe,* meaning "Big River." And so it has remained.

Later Frenchmen moved tentatively but bravely behind Pierre Le Moyne, Sieur d' Iberville, and Jean Baptiste Le Moyne, Sieur de Bienville, La Salle's successors, first to Fort de la Boulaye, near the river's mouth, and eventually to New Orleans in 1718. From that date New Orleans controlled the Mississippi, and control of the Mississippi meant power to dictate the destiny of the whole central continent. No wonder, then, that the river figures in so much of the diplomatic history of the eighteenth century. Spain became master of Louisiana in the treaties of 1762-1763 to guard the approaches to her treasures in New Spain, while Britain at the same time moved to secure her hold on the Illinois by establishing Fort Bute at Bayou Manchac in her newly won West Florida. Small wonder, too, that after independence the young United States would loosen Spain's stranglehold on the Mississippi through the Pinckney Treaty or that she would finally buy New Orleans before necessity compelled her to seize it.

With its absorption into the Union, the lower river moved into the period of its most fabled and romantic history. The earlier trickle of produce from the West now became a flood, as the cargoes of pork, grain, apples, whiskey, flour, bacon, and lead fast began to transform New Orleans into one of the great ports of the world. Now, too, came additional hordes of immigrants to join those earlier refugees from the slave-torn West Indies and revolutionary France—ambitious Americans from the older states and yet more of the displaced from unhappy Ireland and Germany. Some came by the newly invented steamboats, paddling down from the Mississippi's tributaries to the north. But most came by oceangoing ships climbing the twisting river's course from the Gulf.

The trip, then as now, was an experience not soon forgotten. To Frances Trollope the Balize seemed like nothing so much as the very setting for Dante's *Inferno*, and traveler after traveler noted feelings of unease and depression stimulated by this scene which one of them described as epitomizing "the full sublimity of desolation." Such malaise was soon cast aside as the voyagers made the slow ascent to the vibrant metropolis of New Orleans some one hundred miles upstream. Left behind now was the little cluster of laboriously anchored shacks huddled about the base of the Balize lighthouse which marked the southeast pass of the river. Twelve leagues higher, the soil finally congealed into land solid enough to hold Forts Jackson and St. Philip, the first on the west bank, the second on the east bank.

But it was not until the traveler had come to within twenty or thirty miles of New Orleans that the first signs of regular human habitation began to make their appearance. Great earthen levees now fended off the river, and beyond their summits could be seen fields of sugarcane, corn, and rice, dominated by the raised plantation dwelling so typical of the Lower Coast. It usually sat back some two hundred yards from the river, to be approached along a graveled walk which ran from the levee through a large gateway into gardens of spectacular tropical growth and splendor. Built in that indigenous Louisiana style reminiscent of the West Indies, the house sat upon great brick columns which allowed air to circulate freely beneath the living quarters and kept a safe margin between floor and earth, testimony to the unceasing war here against heat and water. The structure itself was almost always of wood, gleaming white in the sunshine. Slender pillars on all sides surrounded wide verandahs protected by Venetian blinds and lattices and strung with hammocks for restful enjoyment of the river breezes.

Beyond the main house lay the service buildings and the slave quarters, usually neat and orderly rows of huts, towered over by the great plantation bell. The fields ran back from the levee for one or two miles, until the

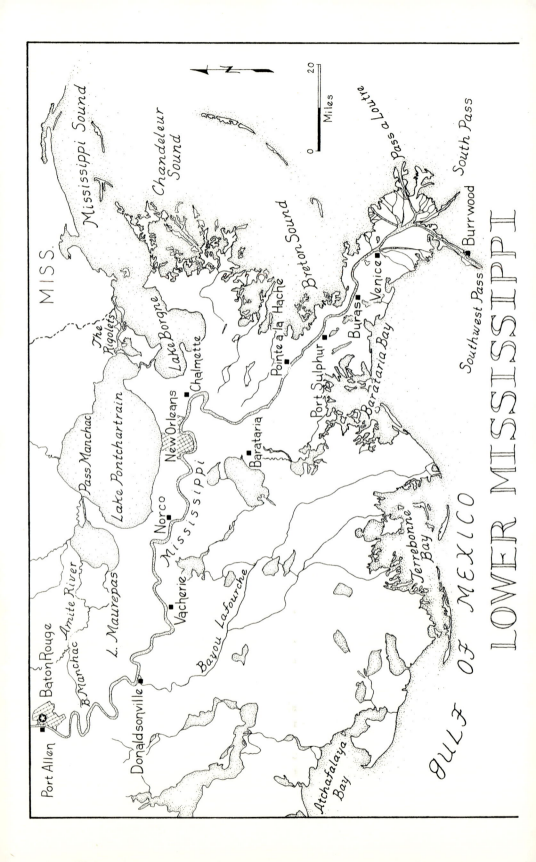

swamps once more held sway. Where cultivation was possible, the lands here were bountiful in corn, rice, tobacco, indigo, and sugar, even too fertile and lush for cotton. Although it would grow along the Lower Coast, cotton, "the white-bud plant," was healthier in the higher upland country.

Topping the levee in front of the estates ran the road to New Orleans, through more and more densely populated countryside, where roses grew in a luxuriance and color matched in few parts of the world. In the river, the ships became more and more numerous as the city was approached, until finally they were vying for position at the crowded docks of the metropolis. It was to the Mississippi that the whole city clung, safe but wary behind its great earthen levees. Nuzzling against these thick embankments were the hundreds of craft which had converged here from all parts of the world. Highest up the river were the rough and vulgar backwoods flatboats and long crocodilelike rafts crowded with the confused array of the foodstuffs of the vast valley. Next came the somewhat more pretentious keelboats, loaded with cotton, furs, liquor, and flour; then the steamboats, by the 1840's the undisputed monarchs of the river, piled with a profusion of cotton bales and heavy cargo; and, finally, the seagoing ships, their masts a dense forest as they crowded, often six-deep, along the wharves.

Finally, strung out above New Orleans were the lavish sugar plantations of the Upper Coast, graced by the imposing mansions which were to become symbols of an age. It was a tragically short age. The haughty steamboats which plied so proudly from plantation landing to market ruled but briefly, though the reign was glittering. At the height of their prowess they carried on the river an annual tonnage greater than that of the combined ships of the British Empire, and in 1849 over a thousand of the big packets pushed up and down the river, floating palaces of sybaritic joys and exhilarating gain.

But the end came quickly, as the railroads began to divert more and more commerce along an east-west axis and away from the old course southward down the river. Civil war brought ruin and destruction, decay of seed crops, dispersion of labor crews, blighting of spirit, and the ignominy of military occupation. And so the region limped along through the late nineteenth century, drowsy and lethargic, dreaming of its past.

Even the river seemed determined to add to the decline. It had always been capricious as it spilled its waters through the many passes at its mouth, favoring now one, now another, closing off here, knifing through a new cut there. By the late nineteenth century the old main-traveled Southeast Pass of bygone days, with its flickering Balize light, had become largely blocked off by a mounting sandbar, and most traffic had shifted to the Southwest Pass and, to a lesser degree, to the South Pass. Prosaic names, these, when compared to those affixed by imaginative deltans to the score or more of smaller passes surrounding them—Octave, Dead Woman, à Loutre, Contrariete, Tiger, Red, Cheniere, Flatboat among them.

Even these two main outlets were silting over in the 1870's, with stubborn sandbars blocking entry or exit and frequently seizing fast to those ships optimistic enough to venture passage. The mighty flow of Mississippi traffic was literally threatened with extinction, and the great port of New Orleans seemed destined for obscurity. Even the steam towboats which had been put to the task of hauling vessels across the bars by sheer force were no answer, and their fees were murderous. In one degree or another the problem had plagued the river since the colonial period, as the troubles of Bienville's engineer, Adrien de Pauger, illustrate.

Over the years the sandbars had been in turn harrowed, dredged, bored with steam-driven propellers, and even dynamited. Nothing had worked, and now the final choking up seemed at hand. It was then that an obstinate ex-Union officer by the name of James B. Eads came upon the scene, fresh from an undisputed victory over the river, his bridge spanning the Mississippi at St. Louis. To the derisive hoots of the professional engineers, this amateur proposed to dredge the passes by using the force of the river itself, channeling its biting current through confining jetties to wash the obstructions out to sea. It worked, of course, first at the South Pass where Port Eads, now a somnolent little village, marks the place of the first feverish construction of the willow mattresses which were sunk to make the jetties. So successful was Eads's project that the United States Army Corps of Engineers took up his process on the more active Southwest Pass; and today Burrwood, at this main entry to the river, continues to house the work of these guardians of its navigation.

Victory over one problem was not victory over them all, and by the twentieth century a pall of another sort began to settle upon the delta. Below New Orleans, where sugar had ruled so long as king, the industry had fallen into decline. Competition had been heightened by the expansion of sugar growing into heretofore unexploited regions of the State, and in an era of new mechanization and centralization of effort easily accomodated along the Upper Coast and in the southwest, the narrow belt of delta land simply could not keep pace. One by one the great plantations died, leaving behind such forelorn, ghostlike remains as "Belle Chasse" and "Orange Grove."

The passing of specialization simply opened the way to the present proliferation and diversity found along the delta. Now the area is the domain of the polyglot mass of small farmers, fishermen, trappers, and fruit growers who had long lived along the lower river and its bayou offshoots, but who in earlier times had been overshadowed by the mighty planters. Here are

Isleños, descendants of Canary Islanders brought over by Spain, still mending nets and singing songs in the fashion of their forebears; Dalmatian "Tockos," Slavic miners of the fabulous oyster beds of the waters around the lower delta; Italian truck farmers and luggermen; French trappers and fishermen; even Chinese, Malayan, and Filipino shrimpers. Buras is today the center of a citrus-growing industry, some of whose produce graces the table as the heady orange wine of the region. Oysters and shrimp, the traditional crops of the sea, have now been outstripped as money catches by menhaden, searched out by low-flying planes radioing their findings to the fleets which will haul their harvest to the processing plant at Empire. Even the muskrat now has a challenger, though the delta still continues to market three times as many of these old familiar pelt-bearers as all other sections of the United States and Canada combined. The amazing fertility of the newcomers, nutrias, leads some to question the wisdom of having brought them in from South America in 1938, but that they are here to stay seems beyond dispute.

Even the trembling earth of the delta is capable of supporting industry. At Port Sulphur, ships haul away brimstone washed up by steaming water from vast deposits deep beneath the marshes some ten miles behind the river. Oil derricks now stretch through swampland and bay, even far out into the Gulf itself, and at Grand Ecaille is found the deepest oil well in the world.

Elsewhere, higher up the Mississippi, change has also come in recent times. World War I revived the heavy cargo traffic on the river, and the creation of the Federal Barge Line shortly thereafter demonstrated the economy of moving such goods as oil, metal, grain, building materials, salt, sulphur, chemicals, and ores in the huge barges which, when lashed together in integrated tows, are now capable of carrying over 35,000 tons of oil, the equivalent of two oceangoing tankers. Modern diesel-powered towboats have succeeded the old lordly steamboats as kings of the river, and if their radio telephones and radar seem to leave little room for the glamor of the old river-pilot days, at least they have succeeded where the old monarchs failed.

No less vital to the new river is the Army Corps of Engineers, who guarantee thirty-foot depth in the Mississippi for the ships making the run to Baton Rouge. This, together with the industrial boom on the Coast, has helped make that city one of the nation's largest inland ports. At Bonnet Carre, in addition, the Corps watches over the great spillway constructed to divert the high waters of the frequently swollen Mississippi into Lake Pontchartrain and out to the sea, thus ruling out the need ever again to breach the levee below New Orleans to save the city, a sacrifice to which the delta was submitted in the early 1920's. Now the Corps can reassure the Lower Coast in other ways as well, not the least being the extensive laying of the great concrete mattresses currently sliding into place all along the levees to shield them from the river's erosive force.

Always it is change, which only highlights the persistence here along the lower Mississippi of so much that the river has created and shaped in the past. Not far from the river's banks men today help build machines to hurl their fellows, hopefully, to the moon. Only a few miles away other men push pirogues as of old along the delta's bayous, telling of *loups-garous* and *feu follets* which dance evilly in the night.

Some are of the future, some are of the past; but, in one way or another, they all belong to the Mississippi.

The Amite to the Tangipahoa

By HODDING CARTER

THIS IS THE STORY of the southeast Louisiana country in which I was born and raised and where a good many of my people have lived.

Men and rivers must alike be considered in relation to the soil which sustains the one and through which the other flows seaward. And so it is not enough to set down that the little rivers of the Florida Parishes run their brief courses dark and swift through the Louisiana enclave that has been known variously to Frenchmen, Spaniards, British, and Americans as French Louisiana, Spanish and British West Florida, the American West Florida Republic, and for the past 150 years as the Florida Parishes of the State of Louisiana. They can be variously identified by their locations and man's designation of them, by their places in history and the uses to which savage and hunter and soldier, trader and settler and wilderness entrepreneur have put them.

So with the rivers of upper southeast Louisiana which rise in the rolling highlands and plunge, meander, or sometimes idle southward between the Mississippi and the Pearl to merge at last with the swamp- and sand-girted Lakes Pontchartrain and Maurepas, which divide the region both topographically and culturally. To the north of the lakes the sons of the Anglo-Saxons and Scots-Irish dominate; to the south the descendants of the French and the Spanish, and latterly the newer Italian, give a Latin imprint. The rivers are the Manchac, the Comite, the Amite, the Tickfaw, the Natalbany, the Tangipahoa, the Tchefuncte, and the Bayou Lacombe. Only one, Bayou Manchac, has a different origin and takes a different direction. The Manchac may once have been a principal channel of the Mississippi river. When the white man came it had been reduced to a springtime freshet which cut its way eastward to a union with the Amite. Today much of it is only a slight indentation.

The tribesmen of the bottomlands, who identified themselves as branches of the great Choctaw tribe, left the rivers and the bordering countryside pretty much as they found them. So, for the white men there were turkey and other game birds, fish, deer, and bear.

The timber westward to near the Amite River was predominantly longleaf pine; beyond, the red oak, the white oak, the pin oak, and the other hardwoods took over. The forests were virginal and at one time were incredibly dense. The rivers flowed through the dense wilderness, and from the branches above them hung heavy in season the clusters of scuppernong and muscadine. Beneath the matted vines the deer drank by the riverside, and foul-smelling alligators slumbered on the sandbars. The streams ran, too, past the scatterings of Indian villages and corn patches; the only erosion came when the risen waters of the springtime fell away from the flooded banks.

The white man intruded upon nature and the Indian more than 250 years ago. Long before then the Spaniard De Soto and the Frenchman La Salle had separately journeyed upon and crossed the Mississippi to keep their trysts with death. The *coureurs de bois* of Canada and other French adventurers from the Old World made up the white vanguard along the lower Mississippi and the Gulf Coast. Then within less than a quarter of a century restless men, mostly soldiers from Biloxi and Mobile and New Orleans and Natchez and Baton Rouge, found the wild country more to their liking than their forts and huts.

The settlements they forsook became the markets for their pelts and surplus foodstuffs, most of the furs to be shipped across the ocean to the mother country. And those who had brought along a wife, or had taken an Indian girl as mate, could eat as well as, and perhaps better than, in the settlements. A woman could tend a few chickens and hogs and even a cow, and plant corn and other vegetables; and all about were wild fruit and berries. When trapping was good a man could bring back from New Orleans, across the lake or from Baton Rouge, little luxuries—wine and sugar, chocolate, and small baubles for children to play with and for a woman to wear at her throat.

From the beginning of the white man's coming, the story of the little rivers is the story of the taking of the land through which the rivers moved—Frenchman from Indian, Britisher from Frenchman, Spaniard from Britisher, and American from Spaniard—to establish here in Spanish West Florida a short-lived and all but forgotten republic.

But in the West Florida country no nation's settlers founded villages that, with the exception of Baton Rouge, grew to be cities. The stamp of the farm and the small town is seemingly indelible. Some of the early river settlements linger on and, modestly, even thrive. But the area really grew with the railroads; the larger towns lie along their tracks. There were prosperous villages before the railroads, of course: Mandeville on Lake Pontchartrain, Covington at the head of navigation on the Bogue Falaya, and Galveztown and Denham Springs on the Amite, and Springfield on the Natalbany, which until the main-line railroads bypassed it could count 2,000 inhabitants. And their emergence was shaped to inescapable ethnic and economic and political patterns. Later would be established other towns along the railroad that ran north and south, with none of them more than six miles from a river: Ponchatoula, Hammond, Independence, Amite, Kentwood, and the others.

Covington grew and persists today because of its timber and medicinal springs, the famed salubrity of the piney-woods "Ozone Belt" and its proximity to New Orleans, of which it has become almost a suburb with the building of the Lake Pontchartrain Causeway.

Galveztown, which came into being because of a military threat, died when the threat no longer existed. Hammond, lying between the Natalbany and the Tangipahoa, grew as a railroad town and a lumber and truck-farming center for which the Illinois Central could provide assured service.

The schooners built in Madisonville plied Lakes Maurepas and Pontchartrain and the small rivers to the north from New Orleans as far as they could ascend, returning with lumber and brick, turpentine and tar. They sailed Bayou Manchac to within a few miles of Baton Rouge long after the little connecting channel to the Mississippi River was filled in by the shovel-wielding troops of Andrew Jackson in 1815 to prevent a British approach to New Orleans from the rear.

The people who lived on the fringes of the lakes and the lower reaches of the little rivers emptying into them did not differ in blood or tongues from their predominantly French and numerically fewer Spanish forebears of New Orleans and Baton Rouge. If only by their presence, they helped in the writing of history. The northern shores of the two connecting lakes and the lower Amite River and Bayou Manchac together formed the border between the New World empires of France and Spain, and for a while Great Britain. And those who dwelt on each side of lake and river were the human proofs of possession.

But it was the Americans who brought political and economic and social and religious change. So the most meaningful story of the rivers of the Florida Parishes is that of the American preemptors.

Few of these Americans who built their cabins along these little rivers were of the tidewater aristocracy; and fewer still cleared out cotton baronies with the labor of their slaves. The feudal landowners were to be found mostly in what would become East Baton Rouge Parish and the East and West Felicianas. Some of the wealthier immigrants, like Leonard Hornsby who settled on the Beaver Creek fork of the Amite River in 1803, even brought their own tailors and shoemakers, along with the more customary blacksmiths, wagonmakers, wheelwrights, and carpenters.

The rest of the parishes were occupied mostly by yeoman white families. More of them came from Georgia and South Carolina than from anywhere else in the young United States, though some of the earliest among them were Tennesseans who had fought under Andrew Jackson at New Orleans and who had found to their liking the rich land of the waving corn, which is the meaning of the tribal name of the land of the Tangipahoa Indians. Almost none of them were of the strata which would later be described with too easy derision as "poor white." Some deteriorated in time, of course, but the newcomers were almost all of solid small-farmer stock, independent and self-sufficient. Their bare hands were skilled, meeting almost instinctively with the plow handle, the woodsman's axe, the paddle of skiff and pirogue, and the hunting rifle. They raised their own foodstuffs and distilled their own whiskey and grazed their own livestock in the oak and magnolia forest and in the piney woods. Sometimes they shot each other out of the saddle, for there were feudists among them, and the bloodletting because of disputes whose origins are forgotten has not altogether come to an end today.

Except for the soon greatly outnumbered descendants of the French and Spanish along the lakes, they were Anglo-Saxon and Scots-Irish and Protestant—almost to a man. The Saxon and Norman names of some of them were already old at Hastings and Runnymede, and those whose ancestors were Scots or Irish or an admixture of both had laid about them with claymore and spiked club and pike at Culloden and the Boyne.

The dogtrot log cabins and the later and roomier clapboard and board-and-batten farmhouses which they built were gracefully utilitarian, some of them habitable and still inhabited today. Near their houses they tapped the pine trees for turpentine, distilling much of it for pitch, and prepared charcoal in woodland kilns, and felled and scaled the pines and oak to be floated or flatboated or borne by schooner to New Orleans. From the underlying clay, which was especially adaptable in present-day St. Tammany Parish, they baked brick for markets farther than New Orleans. No one was rich and few were well to do, but no one went hungry either.

None of the rivers were of the same color or texture along an entire course. At intervals the waters flowed translucent over sand exquisitely fine and white. Along beds and banks of flaming red clay the rivers ran thickly red, only to become a murky black a few miles beyond. Only the sound of running water and the soughing of the forest and the cacophony of small creatures of the wood were the same.

The mainstream of American history brushed but lightly the riverbanks of the Florida Parishes. To that history and to the American destiny two Canadian-French explorers who were brothers, two English military engineers, a Spanish nobleman, and a handful of American rebels against Spain made the most notable contributions, one of them through failure.

Pierre Le Moyne, Sieur d' Iberville, was the oldest brother of a substantial Canadian French family whose parents emigrated to Canada and whose northern seigneuries were not great enough to contain the restless urgings of the family of the Le Moynes. Iberville and his younger brother, Jean Baptiste Le Moyne, Sieur de Bienville, made the Mississippi Valley a French province. Charged by their king to discover and possess the mouth of the Mississippi, they and their companions were the first white men to ascend that river from its mouth. The heart of Iberville, who led the expedition, was in exploration. Bienville, who founded New Orleans in 1718, was the builder.

In his meticulous journal, Iberville described the Frenchmen's momentous first voyage up the river and his own penetration of what would come to be known long after as the Florida Parishes. The brothers planned to rendezvous back at their base at Ship Island in the Gulf of Mexico, hard by the site of the later settlement which the Le Moynes would designate as Biloxi in recognition of the tribe which dwelt along the shore. Bienville was to return to the mouth of the Mississippi and thence northeastward to the island from which they had started out. Iberville would see what he could find in the completely unexplored land to the east and south.

Iberville recorded that on March 23, 1699, he entered near what is now Baton Rouge a subsidiary and minor channel of the Mississippi which the Indians called the Ascantia. Later it and the lower portion of the Amite would be known as the Iberville River and still later as Bayou Manchac, the Choctaw word for "back entrance."

Iberville had two bark canoes, four of his own men, and a Mangoulacha Indian as guide. The stream was so very narrow and so obstructed with fallen trees that in two leagues the party had to make ten portages, and on the second day five times as many. But the explorer was assured by his guide that by this route he could reach the Gulf of Mexico more quickly, so he persisted. What he found on his way was level, beautiful, and heavily wooded country with none of the wild cane which had impeded the voyagers as they camped on the banks of the Mississippi. Although the Mangoulacha guide abandoned Iberville and his men, they paddled on down the Manchac to its union with the wider and far swifter Amite and on into two connected lakes, the first of which Iberville named "Maurepas" and the other "Pontchartrain," in honor of two ministers of the French king. The explorers reached Ship Island several days before Bienville. The guide had been right.

And now for Bienville's contribution. To protect both accesses to the hinterland of France's new empire, he chose to build his colonial capitol at New Orleans which, lying on the banks of the Mississippi, controlled also by a short portage Lake Pontchartrain which lay behind. Thus all sides of what would be known as the Isle of Orleans, bordered by the river, the lakes, and the Gulf, could be protected.

For Lieutenant Philip Pittman and a Captain Campbell of his Britannic Majesty's Army, Bayou Manchac and the Amite would afford neither happy memories nor strategic military success.

The rival nations of the Old World, establishing their titles to the New, contested with each other in the Mississippi Valley from the earliest years of European exploration. In the fall of 1762, Louis XV, Bourbon King of France, gave the Isle of Orleans on the east bank of the Mississippi and his lands west of the river to his Spanish Bourbon cousin, Charles III, in order to keep these possessions out of the hands of the British, with whom he and the French were waging a losing war in Europe and America. Great Britain, by virtue of its victory in the Seven Years' War, expanded its American holdings three months later in the Treaty of Paris to include all of North America with the exception of the Spanish lands west of the Mississippi and the Isle of Orleans on the river's east bank.

Soon after the treaty, young Lieutenant Pittman of the Thirty-fourth Regiment of Engineers was ordered to the Mississippi River to ascertain what could be done to stimulate trade with the Indians, to secure cargo for British bottoms, and to thwart any further Spanish or French ambitions. In time, he recommended that a fort and a warehouse be built at the meeting of the Mississippi River and Bayou Manchac, and that the bayou itself be cleared of the obstructive trees as far back as forty feet from the mean water level and deepened so as to provide a year-round bypass by way of the Iberville River and Lakes Maurepas and Pontchartrain, which would leave New Orleans economically and militarily high and dry. He envisioned that the tribesmen and the white settlers to whom the Mississippi was a trade highway would bring their peltries, tobacco, tallow, and bear's oil to the proposed warehouse in exchange for spiritous liquors, staple groceries, dry goods, and articles needful for their commerce with the savages. The warehouse prospered from the day of its founding, but Lieutenant Pittman's dream of a wide, navigable waterway never became an actuality.

After the lieutenant forwarded his recommendations to his government, Captain Campbell put fifty Negroes to work clearing the Manchac. But, unfortunately, they first cleared the upper end of the bayou at its juncture with the Mississippi. The laborers and their supervisors did not bother to first remove the felled trees and the cane from the all-but-dry riverbed where they had fallen before the axe, nor did they clear the lower segment of the bayou. When the Mississippi rose in the floodtime spring of 1765 before

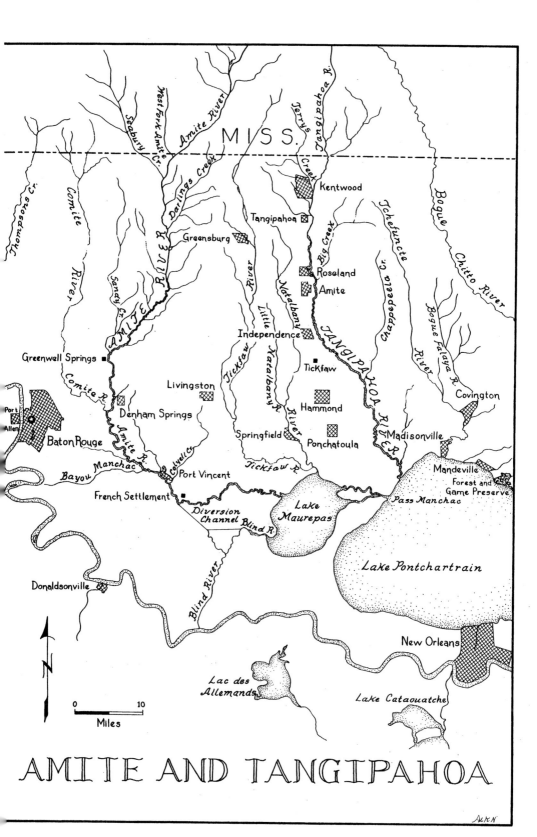

the work was finished, the debris became impenetrable *cheveaux-de-frise*. The congestion was worse than ever before, and the Manchac was never opened to deep-draft or year-round navigation. The plan was not abandoned, however, and the British built their little fort, naming it in honor of their prime minister, "Fort Bute." The soldiers of the Twenty-second Regiment were replaced by redheaded Scots Fusiliers, who intermarried freely with the settlers. Today along Bayou Manchac one finds red-haired men and women of intermingled French and Spanish and Scots descent. And one can discover, too, those who trace their ancestry to German farmers who had come first to Maryland before the Revolution and to Swiss and Germans who moved to the prosperous English settlement from Spanish Louisiana.

And so, in the river and bayou country of the westernmost Florida Parishes, emerged early an amalgam that was unlike the English-speaking Anglo homogeneity to the east.

Now for the story of a grandee of Spain who so humbled the Red Coats in the Mississippi Valley that not until the Battle of New Orleans, thirty-five years later, would England seek by force of arms to regain control of the Mississippi and mid-continental America.

Don Bernardo de Gálvez became governor of Spanish Louisiana in 1777. The young Gálvez proved himself a visionary, courageous, and able colonial administrator. After the American colonists rebelled against their island homeland, the revolutionaries concluded a treaty of alliance and commerce with France which precipitated another of the interminable conflicts between France and England. When Great Britain refused the mediation of Spain, Spain in turn declared war against the British. From this contest she would emerge undisputed owner of both East Florida, which is primarily the State of Florida today, and of West Florida, the name the British gave to the Mobile-based colony they had acquired from France.

Gálvez learned well ahead of the British of West Florida that Spain had recognized the independence of the United States and, from the Spanish commandant at Galveztown, the disposition of British forces. Forthwith, despite one of the worst hurricanes ever to ravage the lower coast, Gálvez persuaded his troops with fervent Latin exhortation to follow him up the river to attack Fort Bute. His 170 Spanish regulars, 330 poor recruits from the Canary Islands, 20 musketeers, 60 militiamen regulars, and 80 free Negroes and mulattoes were joined along the way by 600 volunteers and 160 friendly Indians. Fort Bute was carried by assault, and after a heavy artillery pounding, Gálvez demanded the surrender not only of Fort New Richmond at Baton Rouge but of the town itself and the Natchez District. The British had no choice.

Meanwhile, a sloop fitted out at New Orleans by the American, William

Pickle, captured the large British privateer *West Florida* on Lake Pontchartrain; and Vincent Rieux, a New Orleans Creole, commanding a sloop cruising the lakes, ventured up the Amite River as far as Bayou Manchac. There he placed his fourteen Louisianians in ambush on the riverbank and surprised a heavily armed and laden British barque, with its crew of twelve sailors and fifty Waldeckian officers and grenadiers.

Gálvez afterward moved against Mobile and Pensacola; and, by the Revolutionary War's end, the British had lost the Floridas forever.

The subsequent land deals, by which Louisiana reverted first to France and then was sold to the United States, did not at first affect the administration of the country to the north and east of the Isle of Orleans. West Florida remained in Spanish hands until after rumors began spreading in 1810 that Napoleon was about to seize it. Long before then had begun the breaking of the inexorable American dawn. Anglo-Saxons of both Tory and Rebel sympathies were pushing into West Florida before the American Revolution, paying lip service to Spanish demands that they become Spanish citizens and accept the Roman Catholic faith in exchange for headrights to land. For its part, Spain hoped to create a buffer of these citizens of doubtful loyalty against other American incursors who surely would come later.

Much as the West Floridians disliked Spanish pettifogging and corruption, they were certain they could win more local self-government, possibly even freedom, from Spain more easily than from Napoleon Bonaparte, the tyrannous French conqueror whose power was at its zenith. This conviction helped unite onetime Tory and American. Tory planters, who had settled close by the Mississippi with their slaves, and more recent comers to the east, who had cleared the land with their own hands, began to meet to plan how to take over the region.

Unsure of each other's ultimate political objectives, the leaders found in Freemasonry a common bond and an atmosphere of inviolate secrecy. So, meeting "on the square" in the "five points of fellowship," they began plotting the overthrow of autocratic Spanish rule. On June 23, 1810, they met openly, some five hundred strong, at Buhler's Plains. Though they declared their allegiance to Spain and their opposition to any pretensions of France, they insisted on local self-government and an end to bureaucratic harassment. They set up a provisional administration, at first retaining Don Carlos de Hault de Lassus, the weak Spanish district governor, as governor and first judge. From their own number they selected three associate superior judges, and civil commandants for the Baton Rouge, Bayou Sara, and St. Helena districts. By autumn, the Anglos were ready for open rebellion.

Before dawn on October 22, when the Spaniards in the fort at Baton Rouge parted the gates to admit the cattle which were let out nightly after being milked, a picked group of rebels, lying flat on their ponies, entered the fort with the kine. Victory was won in a matter of minutes. Tragically, one of the two men who died was a young Spaniard who was loved by everyone, Lieutenant Luis de Grand Pré. The other was a Spanish enlisted man.

The American rebels established a brief-lived nation, the West Florida Republic. Miffed because President James Madison had not offered aid for the revolution, they did not request annexation. They named as governor an aristocratic Virginian, Fulwar Skipwith, who traveled this backwoods area in a gilded coach. As commander in chief they picked Philemon Thomas, a rough-tongued storekeeper whose place of business bore the sign in his own lettering "Coughpy fur Sail." One major of volunteers was Isaac Johnson who, immediately after surrender of the fort to the Americans, hauled down the red and yellow Spanish banner, tied it to his horse's tail, and galloped along the dirt streets of Baton Rouge. In the place of the emblem of Spain, the Americans raised a flag of their own which Johnson's wife Melissa had stitched, a single white star on a blue field, whose counterparts one day would wave over Texas and for a while over many of the troops of the embattled Confederate South.

The West Florida Republic lasted seventy-four days. Then Governor W. C. C. Claiborne of Orleans Territory dispatched two small troopships to Baton Rouge and the "bonnie blue flag" was lowered.

Governor Claiborne immediately incorporated what he called Feliciana County into Orleans Territory, and a few months later the country to Pearl River was divided into four parishes: Feliciana; East Baton Rouge; St. Helena, which ran to the Amite and the Tangipahoa; and St. Tammany, named for the New York Indian sachem who was no saint at all, but only a redskinned patriot whom the seaboard recalcitrants had irreverently and lovingly elevated to sainthood. In 1819, Washington Parish was created by cutting off the top of St. Tammany; and, in 1824, Feliciana was divided into two parts. In 1832, Livingston was cut away from the bottom of St. Helena. Not until after the Civil War was Tangipahoa Parish formed from land taken from Washington and St. Tammany to the east and St. Helena and Livingston to the west of the Tangipahoa River.

When Louisiana became a State on July 4, 1812, the West Florida Parishes were included as a part of it.

The people of the Florida Parishes no longer reflect an Anglo or a Latin homogeneity nor are their ways of making their living the same as they once were, though the land nurtures them still. Almost a century ago the farmers began turning increasingly to truck crops and, early in the present century, to dairying and to strawberries, so that the region is all but synonymous with the magnificent crimson fruit it produces. Strawberry culture indirectly wrought prodigious ethnic change.

In the wake of the Civil War and for more than a quarter of a century afterward, Sicilian immigrants came by the thousands to New Orleans, gradually fanning out to the surrounding countryside and in considerable part to the strawberry country. The Sicilians gave a forgotten Old World coloring. Behind the tenant cabins of the large-scale farmers who first gave them work and on the tiny farms which they doggedly acquired, the Sicilians built conical clay ovens for baking bread and milked goats, converting much of the milk into strong, hard cheese, and made sweet, potent wine of the strawberries, and raised garlic and shallots and peppers and tomatoes for their table. On the feast day of St. Joseph, the patron saint of Sicily, even the poorest of them whom the good saint had favored during the previous year decorated their homes with bright paper festoons and strings of peanuts and sweet pastries and opened their doors to anyone who wished to enter and eat and drink and see the children of the family enacting an ancient tableau at the family table in honor of St. Joe.

In time, the sons of the first Sicilians became sizable landowners themselves or opened fruit and vegetable stores and cobbler shops. The sons and grandsons of this second generation are lawyers and doctors, merchants and teachers, and anything else that an ambitious American might want to be.

In lesser numbers came others. Midwesterners with German and Scandinavian names and faces and swart, heavy-shouldered Hungarians. Today all are a part of the American culture which is itself the product of all the cultures that have gone before.

Nor are the rivers the same. The beds of some are dry, or almost so, for a part of the year because of overmuch clearing and draining of land. In places there is unhappy pollution, which need not be. And some run heavy with the clay dregs of the gravel diggings.

The oxteams are gone, as is much of the game; the dogtrot houses are few, and fewer the families who live in them. A persevering man can find a pirogue or a home-fashioned skiff. But, for the most part, the outboard-powered aluminum runabout skims the water in their stead. The squirrel and deer and wild hog and turkey and opossum and succulent raccoon still beckon the hunter. There are heron aplenty yet, and bass and bream and trout and catfish. Once in a blue moon, a huntsman or a fisherman may see an eagle high in a cypress or dark against the sky and, once in a long coon's age, a bear. When I was a high-school student a classmate, a girl, was bitten but not seriously on the cheek by an alligator in the Tangipahoa River while she was splashing alone downstream, away from the rest of us. The alligator retreated, we said, because she was bigger than it was. There was a friend of my father named Chum Anderson who became a local hero after he rammed his arm up a hollow log and pulled out a snarling, raking wildcat. And once Ned McCrady, who is now Vice Chancellor of the University of the South at Sewanee and whose father was the Episcopal rector, had a close call when he dove into the Natalbany to grab a water moccasin to pop its back as you do a whip and the water moccasin popped him in his right big toe instead.

Nowadays, city folk enjoy their weekend lodges and summer houses, and even year-round homes, along the rivers, brought close by the Pontchartrain Causeway and the network of highways. And for those who possess no such place of their own, there beckon the lodges and the natural allures of the State parks.

All in all, a man with only a little imagination can see the vibrant past.

The Pearl

By SIDNEY J. ROMERO

RISING IN EAST-CENTRAL MISSISSIPPI, the Pearl River flows southward, outlines the tip of Louisiana's "toe," divides into the East and the West Pearl rivers, and empties into Lake Borgne and the Rigolets. The last sixty-five miles of its four-hundred-mile-plus journey form a part of the eastern boundary of Louisiana.

From the date of the Louisiana Purchase in 1803, this area, known as West Florida, was a source of contention between Spain and the United States. In 1810, the settlers revolted successfully against the Spanish government, and the area was soon annexed by Louisiana's territorial governor W. C. C. Claiborne on orders of President James Madison.

Many of the Louisiana Creoles were not at all sure that they wanted the Anglo-Saxon settlers of this West Florida as fellow citizens when Louisiana would attain statehood. Therefore, the first act admitting Louisiana as a State, April 8, 1812, ignored West Florida completely. Six days later an act adding the five thousand square miles of West Florida to the infant State was proposed, and its passage allowed the people of the State to vote their minds regarding acceptance or rejection of the addition. From that day to this, Louisiana's eastern boundary has been the eastern mouth of the Pearl River north to the thirty-first degree north latitude and along this parallel to the Mississippi River.

While the Pearl River Basin covers a maximum width of 50 miles and drains an area of 8,760 square miles, that portion which lies within Louisiana extends only from the river itself to the Mississippi River Basin. In Louisiana the Pearl River drains two civil parishes, Washington and St. Tammany, whose eastern boundaries it forms, and the eastern portion of a third parish, Tangipahoa. In this eastern portion of Tangipahoa Parish rises the Tchefuncte River. It flows southward into Lake Pontchartrain and forms an appropriate western terminus for the area to be dealt with here.

From Pearl River on the east, then, to Tchefuncte River on the west is our region. And in this region, as in any other, the land and the people who settled it have so intertwined themselves as to make this a span of space apart, a region different from any other in Louisiana.

Centuries ago Indians made a bid for the romantic for this region when they named the two rivers which bound it Tallahatchie, "river of pearls," and Tchefuncta, "chinquapin." French explorers discovered as early as 1699, however, that the clamlike shells on the floor of the Tallahatchie yielded only worthless pearls, and the dictionary informs us that the chinquapin is simply a "dwarf, shrubby oak."

Honey Island Swamp, a combination salty marsh and jungle in the delta between the East and the West Pearl rivers, provides another tentative link with the romantic. In the nineteenth century it served as refuge for the pirate Pierre Rameau, whose notorious career forms the subject of J. Maurice Thompson's novel, *The King of Honey Island*. Today it is populated only by wild turkeys, deer, fish, and frogs, thus offering unsurpassed fishing and hunting grounds. This offering, however, can be accepted by very few as the entire area is inaccessible except by boat.

Pearls and chinquapins, pirate lair and happy hunting grounds—all are aspects of a romance that might have been. This is the Achilles' heel of the tip of our "toe"; much of it lacks the lure of the picturesque so typical of those adjacent lands which beckon tourists eastward toward Mississippi's Gulf beaches or westward toward New Orleans and/or Cajunland. It is characteristic of our region, though, to dwell not upon weaknesses but upon strengths. Its greatest strength is potentiality deriving from an abundance of resources, both natural and human.

All of Washington Parish and parts of St. Tammany and Tangipahoa lie in the Florida Parish Uplands which, sloping from north to south, have an average altitude of two hundred feet. Here are rolling hills marked by occasional deep gorges, the most scenic of which is Fricke's Cave near Franklinton in Washington Parish. The Bogue Chitto River, the Pearl's principal tributary here; Bogue Lusa, Lawrence, Pushepatapa, and Silver creeks; and numerous swift, clear streams provide an excellent drainage. Their floodplains and creek bottoms combine to produce the land which makes this area one of the State's richest lumber-producing sections.

In the heart of the yellow-pine belt, bordered by forests of ash, hickory, beech, red gum, and white oak, Goodyear interests from Buffalo, New York, established the lumber industry in 1906 by erecting the Great Southern Lumber Company. This company, which became the largest pine sawmill in the world, gave birth to the city of Bogalusa on July 4, 1914. Before it closed its doors, in 1938, it had ensured a long life and a continuous prosperity to the bustling little town by inducing new plants to locate there and by instituting farsighted measures in conservation and reforestation.

Today Bogalusa, the chief manufacturing and trading center of Pearl River Valley, houses Crown Zellerbach and Gaylord Container corporations, outstanding manufacturers of kraft paper, pulp, boxes, bags, and other paper products, and a $500,000 laboratory and a forestry school for experimentation with various species of trees. There are also two chemical companies which convert waste materials into usable products, in addition to approximately thirty-eight other plants. According to the 1960 census, the population was 21,423.

Not only did man make the most of what he found here—use it, conserve it, improve it, and take measures to reproduce it—but a few men of rare foresight and initiative dared to import a new tree from the soil of China and make its cultivation an economic success.

This was the tung, a low, bushy tree with heart-shaped leaves, pink-and-white blossoms in the spring, and a fruit which falls to the ground in the autumn. The fruit yields an oil for use in paint, varnish, waterproofing, linoleum manufacture, and a meal that is used for fertilizer. The first seeds of the tung-nut tree were sent to this country in 1902 by the United States Consul to Kankow, but it was not until the early twenties that the tung potential was visualized by Louisianians.

Walter Green, Sr., who lived near the town of Franklinton, defied ridicule to plant a few acres of tung in cutover pine land. The ridicule turned to envy when the civil war in China hampered production and allowed Green to reap the benefits of his foresight. Unfortunately, it is said that tung products are fighting a losing battle today in competition with the newer synthetics.

Linking this area and its products with the outside world are the Gulf, Mobile, and Ohio Railroad, which ships an average of one hundred carloads of freight per day; two truck and two bus lines; and the Pearl River waterway. The latter could not be counted an asset today were it not for the influence which men have wielded upon this natural resource.

Before the Civil War, Pearl River provided the main artery of transportation from the Gulf of Mexico to Jackson, Mississippi. During the war obstructions were placed in the river to hamper enemy access to Jackson; but, in spite of this, commerce on the river reached its peak in 1895. By 1905, however, the advent of the first railroad line in the parish had spelled fatality to river transportation, with the exception of the floating and rafting of logs to mills near its mouth. Eventually, debris accumulated and the channel deteriorated. But this made little difference to anyone until it was discovered, in the thirties, that sand and gravel deposits on either side of the Pearl could give a lucrative boost to the area's sagging economy.

The Federal Government had been involved intermittently in Pearl River affairs since 1880. Now the River and Harbor Act of 1935 gave the United

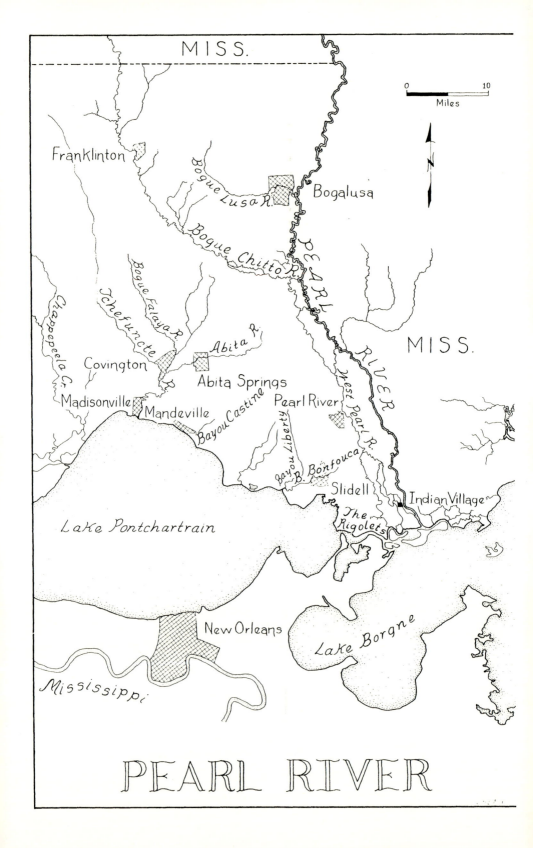

States Army Corps of Engineers the task of making the Pearl navigable. Fifteen years, and over eight million dollars, were required to accomplish this.

Man's knowledge and skill have worked upon nature in the western section of our area, too, where they have produced a near-miracle and a century-old dream come true in the form of the longest overwater highway bridge in the world. The Lake Pontchartrain Causeway, which was completed in 1956 at a cost of $46,000,000, forms a twenty-four mile link between New Orleans and St. Tammany Parish.

Much of St. Tammany Parish is rolling hills, highlands, valleys, and evergreen forests. Much of it, too, is lowlands crossed by bayous which once provided the main method of transportation to Lake Pontchartrain and New Orleans. This part of our area lays claim to more of the picturesque. It claims, too, fishing unsurpassed in both fresh and salt waters. Little wonder that this has been known as a resort area since the early 1800's.

The Marigny de Mandeville family was the first from New Orleans to seek the comfort of summers on the north shore of Lake Pontchartrain. This family built the "Fontainebleau," a large and lovely home named for Louis XIV's country place near Paris. The plantation bell was known far and wide for its mellow tone which, the story goes, was produced by Marigny's addition of one thousand Spanish dollars to the metal while the bell was being cast. At "Fontainebleau" the family entertained lavishly. It is even said that the cigar lighters passed around after one of the dinner parties were one-hundred-dollar bills.

Others from New Orleans came to use the north shore. When it was impossible to find the seclusion necessary for proper dueling in New Orleans, the Creole hotheads would board a steamboat and settle their differences here. Bernard Marigny himself was a duelist. He once challenged a blacksmith and gave him his choice of weapons. Instantly, the blacksmith chose "sledge hammers in six feet of water." Marigny, just under six feet in height, acknowledged defeat with a smile and ordered drinks for all present.

In the 1830's, Bernard conceived the notion of founding a town on the outskirts of his plantation. He divided his holdings into lots and sold them. On July 4, 1834, the Mandeville, an elegant hotel, was opened. It helped to make the little town one of the gayest resort centers in the South.

Marigny next decided to make Mandeville more accessible to New Orleans. He established a direct ferry service between the two shores, providing that no fare should exceed $1.00. Thus, the Lake Pontchartrain Causeway with its $1.00-per-vehicle toll represents a century-old dream come true.

Marigny's plantation continues to provide pleasure—for five thousand persons at a time—for the remains now form the 2,065-acre Fontainebleau

State Park which offers facilities for swimming, hiking, picnicking, and camping, and a sandy beach on the shore of Lake Pontchartrain.

Actually, four of Louisiana's State parks are located within St. Tammany Parish. The newest is Fairview Riverside on the banks of the Tchefuncte River. This park is only two and one-half miles south of Madisonville, a site which lake-voyagers early recognized as ideal for building and repairing ships. For 150 years this little city, which was named unofficially for President James Madison, has built ships, large and small; today it houses two major shipyards.

A few miles up the river is the town of Covington, which stands thirty feet above the Tchefuncte River on one side and the Bogue Falaya on the other. The Bogue Falaya Wayside Park, noted for the charm of its sandy, shady beach, is here, and just a few miles away is Abita Springs Wayside Park, long famed as the place "Where Nature Performs Miracles" by the healing waters which flow, four thousand gallons daily, from nearby springs.

Covington itself was settled by pioneers as early as 1769, and was included in a tract which Jacques Drieux, a New Orleans Creole, bought from the Spanish government in 1803. In 1816, the State Legislature incorporated it, naming it Covington—not, as is popularly believed, in accordance with a label on a Covington Kentucky whiskey keg, but rather in honor of General Leonard A. Covington, a hero of the War of 1812.

Since 1902, the vicinity of Covington has been the site of St. Joseph's Abbey and Minor Seminary. Established by the Benedictines, this was the first permanent seminary in Louisiana.

On Bayou Bonfuca is Slidell, the industrial center of the parish, though it was not settled until after the Civil War. It houses brick and tile factories, sawmills, creosoting plants, and shipyards, one of which produced *Albatross IV,* the Woods Hole oceanographic vessel, in 1964.

It is difficult now to believe that Indians once occupied this entire region. Yet, St. Tammany Parish itself was named for an Indian, though not one of Louisiana. He was Tamened, the Delaware chieftain whose friendship for the whites and whose wisdom in dealing with them led to his "canonization."

In June, 1699, Jean Baptiste Le Moyne, Sieur de Bienville, had headed a peace mission to the Acolapissa Indians (those who listen and see), who lived at what is now Indian Village on the Pearl River about twelve miles from its mouth. There were 1,200 in the tribe at that time, of whom 250 were warriors. In the early 1700's, these Indians moved to a bayou west of Lacombe which they called "Castembouque" (flea) because of the great number of fleas on the banks there.

As the Acolapissas left their area, the Choctaws came from the upper region of the Pearl, in what is now Mississippi, and occupied the St. Tammany wilderness. They had been driven from their homes by the whites; nevertheless, they were as peaceable as the times would permit. They traded freely at the French Market in New Orleans, selling cane baskets, hides, blowguns, and gumbo filé, a seasoning which became an indispensable part of Creole cuisine. Since they spoke the same language as the Acolapissas and intermingled freely with them, it soon became impossible to tell which people belonged to which tribe.

Choctaw or Acolapissa, perhaps the best friend the Indians of this area had was Abbé Adrien Rouquette. Born in New Orleans in 1813, he was said to have been in love with a Choctaw princess who died. Eventually he entered the Catholic priesthood, and in 1859 left New Orleans to do missionary work among the Indians. He built his first chapel near Lacombe and later established another mission, "The Nook," near the same spot. He was so loved by his Indians that they called him "Chata-Ima" (like a Choctaw).

A poet and nature lover, Abbé Rouquette published two books, *Les Savanes, Poesies Américaines*, a collection of poems, and *La Nouvelle Atala*, the story of a young girl who sought happiness by living simply among the Indians.

The Pearl River, legend says, is haunted. Music emanates from its depths in the dark of certain spring nights. Some say this music is the call of Indians who have drowned there. Some say it is the echo of Spanish settlers who marched into the river in order to escape torture and death at the hands of Indians. Some say it is the sound of an orchestra which drowned en route to a performance in New Orleans. Others say it is the spawning song of the gaspergou (freshwater drum).

The legendary music, with its carried rhythms and blended harmonies, forms the perfect background for our region's threefold theme: Land, People, Potentiality.

Baton Rouge, Early 1860's

Harper's Pictorial History of the Civil War

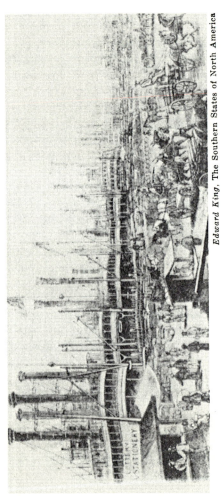

New Orleans Levee, Early 1870's

Edward King, The Southern States of North America

New Orleans, 1862

Harper's Pictorial History of the Civil War

Way's Directory of Western River Packets

New Orleans Wharves, 1890's

New Orleans Chamber of Commerce

Loading Cotton at New Orleans

Louisiana Department of Commerce and Industry

The Port of New Orleans

Greater New Orleans Bridge

New Orleans Chamber of Commerce

New Orleans Chamber of Commerce

Vieux Carre, New Orleans

Sulphur Plant on the Lower Mississippi

Louisiana Department of Commerce and Industry

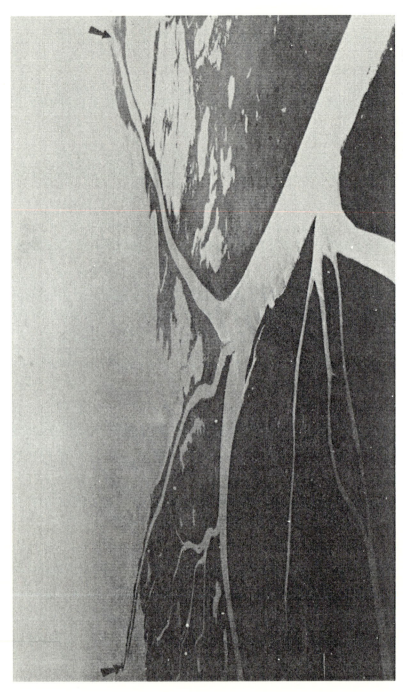

Estuaries of the Mississippi

United States Army Corps of Engineers

Southwest Pass, Mouth of the Mississippi

Louisiana Department of Commerce and Industry

"Mud Lump," Mouth of the Mississippi

Louisiana Department of Commerce and Industry

Meandering Lower Amite River

Louisiana Department of Commerce and Industry

Amite River Diversion Channel

Louisiana Tourist Development Commission

Amite River Near French Settlement

Louisiana Department of Commerce and Industry

Edwin Adams Davis

The Lower Pearl River

Edwin Adams Davis

The Tangipahoa River

Louisiana Department of Commerce and Industry

Paper Mill, Bogalusa

Part VI | Appendix

Biography

HODDING CARTER—*Owner and Editor, Greenville (Mississippi),* THE DELTA DEMOCRAT-TIMES.

B. A., Bowdoin College, Brunswick, Maine; Graduate work, Columbia University, New York, and Harvard University, Cambridge, Massachusetts (Nieman Fellowship). Honorary Degrees include M. A., Harvard University; Doctor of Humane Letters, Washington University, St. Louis, Missouri; Ph. D., Allegheny College, Meadville, Pennsylvania. Guggenheim Fellowship for Creative Writing, 1945; Pulitzer Prize for Editorials, 1946. Editorships: Officer in charge, Middle East edition of *Yank;* Editor, Middle East edition of *Stars and Stripes.* Board Memberships have included: Board of Trustees, Peabody College, Nashville, Tennessee; Board of Overseers, Bowdoin College. Author and coauthor: seventeen books, including *Lower Mississippi; Southern Legacy; Where Main Street Meets the River; Gulf Coast Country* (with Anthony Ragusin); *So Great a Good* (with Betty W. Carter).

ROBERT M. CRISLER—*Professor of Social Sciences and Head, Department of Social Studies, University of Southwestern Louisiana, Lafayette.*

A. B., University of Missouri, Columbia; M. A., Ph. D., Northwestern University, Evanston, Ill. Author: monographs in *The Journal of Geography; Economic Geography; Geographical Review; Missouri Historical Review; The Southwestern Louisiana Journal;* and other professional journals. Former member, Department of Geography, Washington University, St. Louis, Missouri.

EDWIN ADAMS DAVIS—*Professor of History, Louisiana State University, Baton Rouge.*

B. S., Kansas State College at Pittsburg; M. A., State University of Iowa, Iowa City; Ph. D., Louisiana State University. Founder and Former Head, Department of Archives and Manuscripts, and Former Head, Department of History, Louisiana State University. Author: *Louisiana, A Narrative History; Louisiana, The Pelican State; Heroic Years, Louisiana in the War for Southern Independence;* other books and monographs on the history of Louisiana and the South. Founder and Past Managing Editor, *Louisiana History* (Official journal of the Louisiana Historical Association). Past President, Louisiana Historical Association.

SUE LYLES EAKIN—*Instructor of History, Louisiana State University at Alexandria.*
A. B., M. A. (History), M. A. (Journalism), candidate for Ph. D., Louisiana State University. Former journalist. American Association of University Women Research Grant at Louisiana State University, 1962.

☆ ☆ ☆

A. OTIS HEBERT, JR.—*Director, Louisiana State Archives and Records Service, Baton Rouge.*
B. A., University of Southwestern Louisiana, Lafayette; M. A., candidate for Ph. D., Louisiana State University. Former teacher, Louisiana Public Schools; former member, Departments of Social Sciences, Southeastern Louisiana College, Hammond, and Francis T. Nicholls State College, Thibodaux, Louisiana, and Department of History, Louisiana State University. Past Associate Managing Editor and Managing Editor, *Louisiana History* (Official journal of the Louisiana Historical Association).

☆ ☆ ☆

NOLLIE W. HICKMAN—*Professor of History, Northeast Louisiana State College, Monroe.*
B. S., Mississippi Southern University, Hattiesburg; M. A., University of Mississippi, University; Ph. D., University of Texas, Austin. Author: *Mississippi Harvest;* monographs in *Southern Lumberman; Journal of Mississippi History; Louisiana Studies.*

☆ ☆ ☆

MARIETTA M. LEBRETON—*Assistant Professor of Social Sciences, Northwestern State College, Natchitoches, Louisiana.*
B. S., M. A., candidate for Ph. D., Louisiana State University; Seminar for Historical Administrators, Colonial Williamsburg, Williamsburg, Virginia, 1960. Book reviews published in *Louisiana History; The Journal of Mississippi History; Louisiana Studies.*

☆ ☆ ☆

WALTER M. LOWREY—*Professor of History, Centenary College of Louisiana, Shreveport.*
B. A., M. A., Louisiana State University; Ph. D., Vanderbilt University, Nashville, Tennessee. Former member, Department of Social Sciences, and Dean, Division of Arts and Sciences, Francis T. Nicholls State College, Thibodaux, Louisiana. Author: monographs on history of Louisiana. Past President, Louisiana Historical Association.

☆ ☆ ☆

ADA L. K. NEWTON—*Drafting Assistant, Geology Department, and Ph. D. Candidate, Louisiana State University, Baton Rouge.*
B. A., Pan American College, Edinburg, Texas; M. A., Texas College of Arts and Industry, Kingsville, Texas. Art and history instructor, Texas High Schools, 1956-59, 1961-64; University of New Mexico Anthropology Museum Field Work, 1960; Assistant, Geology Department, Louisiana State University, 1964. Published cartography in J. Preston Moore, *The Cabildo in Peru Under the Bourbons*, (Durham, N. C., 1966).

☆ ☆ ☆

SIDNEY J. ROMERO—*Professor of Social Sciences and Head, Department of Social Sciences, Southeastern Louisiana College, Hammond.*
B. A., University of Southwestern Louisiana, Lafayette; M. A., Ph. D., Louisiana

State University; Postdoctoral study, University of Southern California, Berkeley. Former member, Department of History, Oklahoma State University, Stillwater; Department of History, Louisiana State University.

☆ ☆ ☆

RALEIGH A. SUAREZ—*Professor of History and Dean of the Division of Humanities, McNeese State College, Lake Charles, Louisiana.*
B. S., M. A., and Ph. D., Louisiana State University. Former teacher, Louisiana Public Schools; and member, Department of History, Louisiana State University. Author: monographs on the social and economic history of Ante Bellum Louisiana. Past President, Louisiana Historical Association.

☆ ☆ ☆

JOE GRAY TAYLOR—*Professor of Social Sciences, McNeese State College, Lake Charles, Louisiana.*
B. A., Memphis State University, Memphis; M. A., Ph. D., Louisiana State University. Author: *Negro Slavery in Louisiana; Louisiana, A Student's Guide to Localized History;* several books dealing with United States Air Force history; monographs on the history of Louisiana and the South. President, Louisiana Historical Association. Past President, Louisiana Historical Association.

☆ ☆ ☆

JOSEPH G. TREGLE, JR.—*Professor of History, Louisiana State University in New Orleans.*
B. A., Loyola University, New Orleans, Louisiana; M. A., Louisiana State University. Ph. D., University of Pennsylvania, Philadelphia. Past Dean of Academic Affairs, Louisiana State University in New Orleans, 1959-1964. Author: monographs on history of Louisiana. Past editor, *Louisiana Historical Quarterly* (Official journal of the Louisiana Historical Society). Past President, Louisiana Historical Association.

☆ ☆ ☆

PHILIP D. UZEE—*Professor of History and Dean of the Division of Arts and Sciences, Francis T. Nicholls State College, Thibodaux, Louisiana.*
A. B., M. A., and Ph. D., Louisiana State University. Former member, Department of Social Sciences, McNeese State College, Lake Charles, Louisiana; and Department of History, Louisiana State University.

☆ ☆ ☆

JOHN D. WINTERS—*Professor of History, Louisiana Polytechnic Institute, Ruston.*
B. A., M. A., Ph. D., Louisiana State University. Special Study, Rollins College, Winter Park, Florida; Graduate Study, Harvard University, Cambridge, Massachusetts. Author: *The Civil War in Louisiana* (Louisiana Library Association Certificate of Merit, "the most distinguished book on Louisiana published during 1963"). President, Louisiana Historical Association.

Index

Acadians, 113; settling of, on Bayou Lafourche, 122. *See also* Cajuns
Acolapissa Indians, 170, 171
Adams-Onis Treaty, 83, 88–90
Alabamu Indians, 108
Alden, Issac, 46
Alexandria, 28, 54, 55, 60, 61, 107
Allen Parish, 90
American, newspaper, 92
American Revolution, 160, 161
Americans, 55; in southeast Louisiana, 155–56
Amite River, 153, 154, 156, 161, 162
Anderson, Chum, 163
Anglo-Saxons, 28, 154, 165. *See also* Anglos
Anglos, 160, 161, 162, 165. *See also* Anglo-Saxons
Anilco Indians, 23
Anilco River, 23
"Arcadia," plantation, 107
Arceneaux, Louis, 107
Archimedes, Shreve's snag boat, 55, 56
Arkansas, 14, 21
Arroyo Hondo, 82. *See also* Rio Hondo
Ascension Parish, 121, 122
Assinai Indians, 87
Assumption Parish, 121, 122
Atchafalaya Basin, 113, 119
Atchafalaya River, 52, 105, 107, 108; description of, 114; discovery and early days of, 113; flood-control plan for, 114–15; role of, in modern commerce, 120; showboats on, 118; steamboats on, 116; threat of, 114; wilderness of, 115, 118–19, 120
Atkinson, Brig. Gen. Henry, 88
Attakapa Indians, 87, 108
Audubon, John James, 16
Austin, Stephen F., 56
Avoyelles Parish, 105
Avoyelles plain, 55

Bailey, Lt. Col. Joseph, 60, 116

Bal ce soir, 124
Balize, the, 147, 149
Banks, 92
Banks, Capt. Fred, 20
Banks, Capt. Jack, 20
Banks, Gen. Nathaniel P., 59, 60, 116; at Port Hudson, 10; invades Teche country, 110
Barnett, James, 88
Bartholomew, Bayou, 22
Bastrop, Felipe Enrique Neri, Baron de, 21, 26; colonization by, 24
Bastrop, La., 28
Baton Rouge, 5, 6, 11, 143, 144, 154, 155, 160; capture of, by West Florida rebels, 161–62
Battles. *See* place name
Baudier, Roger, 87
Bayous. *See* principal name
Beauregard Parish, 78, 79, 90
Bienville, Jean Baptiste Le Moyne, Sieur de, 21, 23–24, 54, 122, 146; founds New Orleans, 157, 158; heads mission to Acolapissa Indians, 170; Mississippi River explorations of, 157
Bilbo, Thomas, 88
Biloxi, Miss., 143, 157
Bisland, Battle of, 110
Bistineau, Lake, 45, 46, 47, 49, 53
Black Bayou, 46, 127, 128
Black, Lake, 53
Black River, 14, 27, 52; formation of, 22; source of, 21
Blue, Bayou, 127
Bodcau Lake, 53
Boeuf, Bayou, 53, 55, 105
Boeuf River, 22, 26; source of, 21
Bogalusa, 167
Bogue Chitto River, 166
Bogue Falaya River, 155, 170; Wayside Park, 170
Bonaparte, Napoleon, 82, 161
Bonfuca, Bayou, 170
Bonne Idee Bayou, 21

Bonnet Carre Spillway, 151
Boré, Etienne de, 7
Borgne, Lake, 165
Bossier City, 57
Bowie, James, 21; story of, 107
Bowie, Rezin, Jr., 107
Bragg, Gen. Braxton, 126
Brashear City, 86, 116; in Federal invasion of Teche country, 110. *See also* Morgan City
British, 160, 161
Bruin, Lake, 5
Bryan, John, 90
Bryan, J. W., 90

Caddo Indians, 23, 45, 46, 54
Caddo Lake, 53
Cajuns, customs and character of, 112; origin of, 106; in Teche country, 111–12. *See also* Acadians
Calcasieu Lake, 85, 86, 90, 93
Calcasieu Parish, 78, 79, 88; formation of, 90
Calcasieu Pass, 86
Calcasieu River, 78, 82, 90, 93; commerce on, 85–86; obstacles in, 86; origin and description of, 85; regional characteristics in area of, 91; settlement of, 88, 89
Cameron Parish, 78
Campbell, Capt., attempts to clear Bayou Manchac, 158
Camp Sabine, 83
Campti, 56, 60
Cane River Lake, 53
Cantonment Atkinson, 88
Carondelet, Francisco Luis Hector de Noyelles, Baron de, 24
Carron, Bayou, 105
Cary, Sylvester L., 92
Cass, Lewis, 55
Catahoula Lake, 22
Cathart, James Leander, first to report Atchafalaya, 113
Catholic Church in America, The, 87
Cattle, 13; industry, 91
Charenton, 105, 108, 119
Charles Lake, 88; naming of, 90
Charles III, 158
Chevaux-de-frise, 160
Chitimacha Indians, 122; in Teche country, 108
Choate, David, 90
Choctaw Indians, 108, 153–54, 170–71
Civil War, 7, 8, 18, 21, 59, 85, 167; on Atchafalaya River, 116; effect of, on river transportation, 27; effects of, in Tensas Basin, 18, 19; invasion of Teche country during, 110
Claiborne, W. C. C., 162, 165
Clark's Bayou, 45
Clemens, Samuel, 143
Cocodrie, Bayou, 105; Swamp, 5, 8
Coffee, Cajun, 111, 112

Comite River, 153
Concordia, Lake, 5
Concordia Parish, 6, 13; land grants in, 15
Confederacy, 10; Federal expedition against, in Red River Valley, 59–60
Confederates, in Federal invasion of Teche country, 110
Cooley, C. B., 20
Corn, 8, 59, 123, 147, 149
Corney Lake, 22
Cotton, 13, 55, 59, 60, 123; cultivation of, 7, 8, 12, 18; decline of, 29; along Lower Coast of Mississippi River, 149
Cotton Valley, 50, 51
Coureurs de bois, 154
Courtableau, Bayou, 105, 107
Coushatta Indians, 87
Covington, 155; founding of, 170
Covington, Gen. Leonard A., 170
Crawfish, 119; Festival, 106
Crockett, Davy, 56, 107
Cross Lake, 53
Crozat, Antoine, 24
Cumberland River, 6

D'Arbonne, Bayou, 22
Darby, William, 46
Davis Island, 5
Davis, Jefferson, 5
Davis, Joseph, 5
De l'Outre, Bayou, 22
Delta, of Mississippi River, 144–45; present-day industry on, 150–51
De Soto, Hernando, 21, 146, 154; discovers Tensas River, 15; explorations of, 22–23
DeSoto Parish, 78, 79
Destruction and Reconstruction, 105
D'Iberville. *See* Iberville
D'Inde, Bayou, 88
Donaldsonville, 121, 122, 124, 126, 127, 144
Dorcheat, Bayou, origin of, 45; settlement of, 45–46; steamboats on, 47
Dowling, Richard W., 83
Drew, Newt, 46, 49
Drieux, Jacques, 170
Du Large, Bayou, 127
Dutch Town. *See* Germantown

Eads, James B., plan of, to dredge Mississippi River, 150
East Baton Rouge Parish, 155, 162
East Carroll Parish, 13
East Feliciana Parish, 155, 162
Emma, trading sloop, 85
Enterprise, steamboat, 7, 56
Evangeline, story of, 106–107

Fabacher, Joseph 92
Fais-dodos, 112, 125–26. *See also* bal ce soir.

INDEX 197

False River, 5
Farming, by settlers in northeast Louisiana, 16
Farms, of Acadians, 123
Federal Barge Line, 151
Federal Government, 114, 167–68. See also United States
Federals, invade Lafourche country, 126; invade Teche country, 110. See also Union
Filhiol, Don Juan, 24
Fishing, 13, 16, 20, 51, 120, 151, 163, 166, 169; on Atchafalaya River, 115; at Melville, 118
Flood Control Act of 1928, p. 114
Flood of 1927, pp. 14, 114
Florida Parishes, 153, 155, 157, 160; changes in ethnic composition of, 163
Florida Parish Uplands, 166
"Fontainebleau," 169
Forests, 119. See also Timber
Fort Beauregard, 27
Fort Bute, 146, 160; Gálvez's victory at, 160
Fort de la Boulaye, 146
Fort Jackson, 147
Fort Jesup, 83
Fort Miró, 24, 26
Fort New Richmond, 160
Fort Rosalie, 24
Fort St. Philip, 147
France, 24, 81, 82, 161; occupation of Louisiana by, 15
Francis T. Nicholls State College, 111, 121
Franklin, Battle of, 110
Franklin, Gen. William B., in invasion of Teche country, 110
French, 24; language, 111–12, 123
French and Indian War, 6
Fresh water, 79
Frisby, Norman, 18–19
Fur, animals on Atchafalaya, 119; muskrat and nutria, 151

Galveston, Texas, 86
Gálvez, Bernardo de, 108, 127; victories of, against British, 160, 161
Galveztown, 155, 160
Germantown, establishment of, 49, 50
Golden Meadow, 121, 123, 126, 127
Goodwin (Gordon) Shoals, 78
Goos, Capt. Daniel, 91
Grand Calliou Bayou, 127
Grand Lake, 110, 120, 122
Grand Pré, Lt. Luis de, 162
Grant, Gen. Ulysses S., 10
Great Britain, 146, 160; expands American holdings, 158
Great Raft. See Red River
Green, Brig. Gen. Thomas, leads Confederates at Battle of Bayou Bourbeau, 110

Green, Walter, Sr., 167
Guachoya Indians, 23
Gulf Coast, 87, 154, 143
Gunboats. See Riverboats
Guyers Bayou, 19

Hammond, 155
Harpe brothers, 7
Hebert, Alexander, 90
Henderson, John, 90
Hodges, James, 90
Honey Island Swamp, 166
Hornsby, Leonard, 155–56
Houma, 128
Houston, Sam, 56
Hun, David, 18
Hunting, 13, 15, 20, 51, 119, 166

Iberville, Pierre Le Moyne, Sieur d', 122, 146; Mississippi River explorations of, 157
Iberville River. See Manchac, Bayou
Iles, Dempsey, 90
Indians, 15, 87, 146, 154, 170, 171; in Boeuf and Ouachita valleys, 22; Mangoulacha guide of Iberville, 157; of Teche area, 108. See also tribal name
Industrial Canal, 144
Industry, 29; north of Baton Rouge, 13
Intracoastal Canal, 122
Isle of Orleans, 158

Jackson, Andrew, 8, 155
Jackson, Miss., 10, 167
James, Frank, 28
James, Jesse, 21, 28
Jefferson Davis Parish, 90
Joes Bayou, 18, 19
Johnson, Isaac, 162
Johnson, Joshua, 90
Johnson, Melissa, 162

King of Honey Island, The, 166
Kirby, Samuel Adams, 91
Kleinpeter, Thomas, 92
Knapp, Seaman A., 92
Knights of the White Camelia, 28
Koasati Indians, 87
Kock's Plantation, 126
Krotz Springs, 118, 119

Labiche, Emmeline, 107
Laborde, Ennos, family, 16
Lacombe, Bayou, 153
Lafayette (Vermilionville), 108, 111, 112
Laffite, Jean, 88, 107
Lafourche, Bayou, 21; Acadian culture on, 123; damming of, 124; description of, 121–22; industries on, 123; recreation on, 124–26; saints of region, 127; settlement pattern of, 127; steamboats on, 123–24

Lafourche country, Federal invasion of, 126; settling of, 122
Lafourche Parish, 121
Lake Charles (city), 85, 86, 87, 90, 91, 92, 93; present-day importance of, 93
Lake Pontchartrain Causeway, 155, 164, 169
La Nouvelle Atala, 171
Larto Lake, 105
La Salle, René Robert Cavelier, Sieur de, 21, 23, 54, 113, 146, 154; explorer of the Mississippi River, 6
Lassus, Don Carlos de Hault de, 161
LeBleu, Martin, 88
Leeville, 105, 121, 126
Leon, Bernhard Muller, Count, founds Germantown, 49–50
Les Rapides, 54, 55
Les Savanes, Poesies Américaines, 171
Little Bayou Black, 128
Little River, 14, 22, 27
Livingston Parish, 162
Loggy Bayou, 45, 46, 47, 50
Los Adaes, Presidio del Nuestra Señora del Pilar de, 54, 82
Louis XIV, 146
Louis XV, 158
Louisiana, 5, 10, 16, 21, 26, 45, 79, 80, 82, 83, 87, 112, 113, 122, 146, 165; boom in southwest of, after Reconstruction, 91, 92; in Civil War, 116; Indians in, 6, 108; southeast, 153, 154, 155, 156; transferred to United States, 24
Louisiana Purchase, 6–7, 87, 163
Louisiana State Legislature, 90, 170
Louisiana State University, 112
Louisiana Wild Life and Fisheries Commission, 119
Lower Coast, of Mississippi River, 147, 149, 152; industrial boom on, 151
Lumber industry, 50, 85, 86; in Calcasieu River region, 91; in Florida Parish Uplands, 166. *See also* Sawmills; Timber
Lynch, Charles, 26

McClanahan Shoals, 77–78
McCrady, Ned, 164
McNeese State College, 93
Macon, Bayou, 14, 15, 18, 19, 21; riverboats in area of, 19, 20; role of, in commerce, 20
Madison Parish, 13, 19, 27
Madison, President James, 165, 170
Maison Rouge, Joseph, Marquis de, colonization by, 24
Manchac, Bayou, 146, 153, 155, 158, 161; attempt to clear, 158–60; changing names of, 159; ethnic composition of territory along, 160
Mandeville, 169
Mariecroquant, Bayou, 105

Marigny, Bernard, founds Mandeville, 169
Marigny de Mandeville, family, 169
Marquette, Father Jacques, 146
Mason, Samuel, 7
Maurepas, Lake, 153, 155, 157, 158
Melville, 116–18
Memphis, Tenn., 10
Mena, Brother Marcos de, 87
Menard, Father Charles M., 127
Mexico, 6, 54, 59
Mexico, Gulf of, 6, 23, 77, 78, 120, 144, 145, 157, 167
Midwesterners, 91
Miller, Capt. John, 86
Minden, 46, 50, 51; founding of, 49
Minden Academy, 49
Miró, Esteban, 24
Mississippi River, 5, 13, 14, 23, 52, 108, 113, 114, 116, 122, 124, 154, 158–60; boats on, 147, 149, 151, 152; in Civil War, 10; "Coast" of, 143–44; colonial homes on, 144; commerce, 147, 149; deep delta of, 144–45; description of, 143; exploration of, 6, 146, 157; importance of, to nation controlling, 146; industry on, 144, 150–51; sandbars in, 150; settlement on, 8; squatters on, 16; traffic on, 6–7, 12; underwater inhabitants of, 146; wartime destruction on, 11. *See also* Lower Coast; Upper Coast
Mississippi, State of, 5
Mississippi Valley, 157
Monroe, 14, 24, 26, 27, 28
Morehouse Parish, 24, 27
Morgan City (Brashear City), 108, 115, 120
Morhouse, Abraham, 26
Morse, Peabody Atkinson, founds Ninock, 50
Moscoso, Luis de, 23, 146
Moss, Henry, 88
Mounds, 22
Mouton, Brig. Gen. Alfred, Confederate leader, 110
Murrell, John, settler of the Dorcheat, 46
Murrell, John A., outlaw, 7
Musco, Lucien, 127
Muskrat, 151

Nana, Bayou, 78
Narváez, Pánfilo de, 146
Natalbany River, 153, 155
Natchez Indians, 6, 15, 23, 24
Natchez, Miss., 5, 6, 7, 8
Natchitoches, 54, 55, 56, 82, 83
Negreet, Bayou, 78
Neutral Ground, 82–83, 90
Neutral Strip. *See* Neutral Ground
Neville, Margarite, 107
New Iberia, 108

INDEX

New Orleans, 7, 8, 10, 27, 55, 60, 144, 146, 147, 149, 150, 151, 169, 171; building of, 158; industrial boom at, 144
New Orleans, steamboat, 7
Nicholls, Francis T., 126
Ninock, founding of, 50
No Man's Land, 88. *See also* Neutral Ground
Nutrias, 151

Ohio River, 6
Oil, 13, 151. *See also* Petroleum
Ojibway Indians, 146
Old River, 5, 114
Old Spanish Trail, 120
Olmstead, Frederick Law, 59
Opelousas, 91, 107
Opelousas Indians, 108
Orange, Texas, 77
Orleans Territory, 162
Ouachita River, 14, 22, 24, 26, 27, 52; source of, 21
Overton, 46; rise and decline of, 49

Parker, Webb, family, 16
Parks, State, 164, 169–70
Pauger, Adrien de, 150
Pearl River, 166, 170, 171; during Civil War, 167; commerce on, 167; course of, 165; made navigable, 167–68
Pearl River Basin, 165
Pearl River Valley, industry in, 167
Perrin, William Henry, 91
Petit Calliou Bayou, 127
Petroleum, 13, 79, 108, 120, 151; on Atchafalaya, 119; along Dorcheat, 50–51. *See also* Oil
Pickle, William, 160–61
Pinckney Treaty, 147
Pineda, Alonzo Alvarez de, 146
Pittman, Lt. Philip, recommendations of, 158
Plantations, cotton, 18; destruction of, during Civil War, 11; description of, on Lower Coast, 147–48; life on, 8; sugar, 128, 144, 150
Plaquemine, Bayou, 107
Pleasant Hill, Battle of, 60
Pointe Coupee Parish, 8, 13
Polk, Leonidas, 126
Pontchartrain, Lake, 144, 151, 153, 155, 157, 158, 161, 163, 169, 170
Population, of Ouachita-Boeuf region, 29; of Sabine River area, 78–79; makeup of, in Teche country, 110–11
Port Hudson, 10, 11, 59, 126–27
Porter, Adm. David, 59
Praither, William, 90
Providence, Lake, 5, 10, 14

Railroads, 28, 29, 57, 60, 149; in Calcasieu River area, 86; Gulf, Mobile, and Ohio Railroad, 167; Illinois Central, 155; in Pearl River area, 167; Red River Line, 60; of southeast Louisiana, 154–55; Southern Pacific Railroad, 86, 91; in Teche country, 108; Texas and Pacific Railroad, 60; Watkins Railroad, 92
Rameau, Pierre, 166
Rapp, George, 50
Reconstruction, 21, 28; end of, 11–12; for Louisianians, 11; Acts, 11
Red River, 5, 8, 10, 21, 27, 45, 46, 47, 55, 61, 105, 108, 114; exploration of, 54; Great Raft of, 53, 55–56, 57, 58; navigation on, 57–59, 60; origins of, 52; settlement of, 54, 55; steamboats on, 57–59; waters of, 57
Red River Campaign, 116
Red River Valley, 110
Red River Valley Association, 61
Reon, Louis, 88
Rice, 20, 92, 123, 147, 149
Richland Parish, 27
Rieux, Vincent, 161
Rio Grande, 82, 87, 88
Rio Hondo, 87, 88. *See also* Arroyo Hondo
River and Harbor Act of 1935, pp. 167–68
Riverboats, 7, 26, 120, 124; on Calcasieu River, 85, 86; gunboats, 27, 126; on Mississippi, 149, 151, 152; on Red River, 59; showboats on Atchafalaya, 118; on southeast Louisiana rivers, 155; steamboats, 12, 26, 27, 47, 55, 57–59; 108, 116, 123–24, 147, 151; on Tensas-Bayou Macon, 20; in Tensas Basin, 19
Roads, 27–28, 29, 59, 91; El Camino Real, 56, 83; River Road, 144
Roman Catholic Faith, 161; in Teche country, 111; in Lafourche country, 123
Roundaway Bayou, 18, 19
Rouquette, Abbé Adrien, 171
Ryan, Jacob, 88
Ryan, Jacob, Jr., 90, 91

Sabine Lake, 77, 78
Sabine Parish, 78, 79
Sabine Pass, 77, 78
Sabine River, 83, 84, 87–88; description of, 77–78; importance of, 80; mapping of, 82; navigation on, 78; role of, in economic development, 79
Sabine Valley, 78, 82, 84
St. Amico, 127
Saint-Denis, Louis Antoine Juchereau de, 21, 23–24, 54
St. Helena Parish, 162
St. James Parish, 122
St. John, Lake, 5
St. Joseph, Lake, 23

INDEX

St. Joseph's Abbey and Minor Seminary, 170
St. Landry Parish, 90, 108
St. Louis, Mo., 27
St. Tammany Parish, 162, 165, 166, 169, 170; State parks in, 169–70
St. Valerie, 127
Sallier, Charles, 90
Sandbars, in Mississippi River, 150
Santa Anna, Antonio López de, 88
Santa Rosa Island, 143
Sawmills, in Dorcheat region, 50
Sharecropping, 11, 12
Shreve, Capt. Henry Miller, 55, 57, 114; designs shallow-draft steamboat, 19, 26; removes Great Raft, 55–56
Shreveport, 53, 61, 59–60; incorporation of, 56–57
Sibley, Dr. John, 46, 55
Sicilians, in New Orleans area, 163
Simmesport, 115, 116, 120
Skipwith, Fulwar, 162
Slaves, 18; during Civil War, 11; life of, on plantations, 8
Slidell, 170
South Pass, 149, 150
Southeast Pass, 149
Southwest Louisiana, Biographical and Historical, 91
Southwest Pass, 150
Southwestern Louisiana, University of, 111, 112
Spain, 6, 7, 23, 54, 55, 81, 82, 87, 146, 160, 165; occupies Louisiana, 15–16
Squatters, life of, 16
Steamboats. See Riverboats
Strawberry culture, influence of, 162–63
Streck, Capt. F. N., 123
Sugar, 13, 59, 149; plantations, 128, 144, 150. See also Sugarcane
Sugarcane, 147; cultivation of, 7–8; on Bayou Lafourche, 123; on Teche, 106. See also Sugar
Sulphur, discovery of, 92
Sulphur, La., 92
Swamp Land Act of 1850, p. 18

Tallahatchie River, 166
Tallulah, 5, 19
Tamened, Delaware chieftain, 170
Tangipahoa Parish, 162, 165, 166
Tangipahoa River, 153, 162, 163
Taylor, Gen. Richard, 60, 105; commands Confederates in Teche invasion, 110
Tchefuncte River, 153, 165, 166, 170
Teche, Bayou, description of, 105; settlement pattern on, 105–106; steamboats on, 108
Teche country, Federal invasion of, 110; population makeup of, 110–11

Tensas Basin, 14, 15, 23; effects of Civil War in, 19; plantations in, 18; settlement in, 15–16
Tensas Indians, 15, 23
Tensas Parish, 5, 13
Tensas River, 16, 18, 22, 27, 105; discovery of, 15; origin of, 14; riverboats on, 19, 20; role of, in commerce, 20
Terrebonne, Bayou, 127, 128
Terrebonne Parish, 127; bayou settlement pattern of, 128
Texas, 10, 11, 83
Thevenet, Andrew, 106
Thibodaux, 127
Thomas, Philemon, 162
Thompson, J. Maurice, 166
Thomson, Alexander, 92
Tickfaw River, 153
Timber, on Atchafalaya, 120; of northeast Louisiana, 16; of southeast Louisiana, 154, 155. See also Forests; Lumber industry; Sawmills
Toledo Bend Dam, 79–80, 83, 84
Tonti, Henri de, 6, 52, 54, 113, 161
Treaty of Paris, 158
Trembling earth, 145; industry on, 151
Trollope, Frances, 147
Tung tree, culture of, 167
Tunica Indians, 6, 23

Union, army on Atchafalaya River, 116; attempts to gain control of Texas, 83; expedition of, in Red River Valley, 59–60. See also Federals
United States, 87, 122, 146–47, 151, 165; offers homesteads, 90. See also Federal Government
United States Army Corps of Engineers, 13, 55, 57, 114, 115, 150, 151–52, 167
United States Navy, 113
Upper Coast of Mississippi, 149, 150

Veeder, Charles L., 49
Vermilionville, 91, 110. See also Lafayette
Vernon Parish, 78, 79
Vicksburg, Miss., 5, 8, 10, 11, 14, 28, 59; Grant at, 10
Vidal Bayou, 18, 19
Vidal, Joseph, 6
Vincent, Pierre, 88, 90

Washa Indians, 122
Washington Parish, 162, 165, 166
Watkins, Jabez B., part of, in development of Calcasieu country, 92
Wauksha, Bayou, 105
Webster Parish, 49, 51
West Baton Rouge Parish, 8
West Carroll Parish, 24, 27

West Feliciana Parish, 5, 155, 162
West Florida, 6, 7, 146, 154, 161, 165; American rebellion in, 161–62; Republic, 162
West Florida, British privateer, 161
West, Richard, 90
White, Edward Douglass, 126–27
Wildlife, on Atchafalaya River, 115, 119; in Florida Parishes, 163; waterfowl of Mississippi delta, 145–46
Williamson, Capt. Thomas Taylor, 57
Woodruff, Lt. E. A., 57
Woodworth, Comm. S. E., 27

Yellow fever, on Bayou Lafourche, 126
Younger brothers, 21, 28

Printed in the United States
1323600005B/223-246